LESSONS FROM A NONCUSTODIAL FATHER

by

J. P. Allen

INTRODUCTION

Good day reader. I am going to share my experiences in Fatherhood. Successes and failures for those who may be dealing with these same issues I will be focusing on in this book. I am a Father first. Have been both custodial and noncustodial parent. Also a child of divorce who lived in the child's point of view. So there isn't much that I can't make you aware of. The reason for this book is to give you a guide of things to do and things to look out for when you are co-parenting with someone who may or may not be cooperative.

My reasoning for this guide is simple. In an ideal world parents should share an equal amount of time raising a child. But this isn't an ideal world. Mother's win custody of children 9 out of 10 times in the court system, yet kids seem to be worse off as the years go by. Kids are increasingly lacking skills, manners, ambition, confidence, common sense, respect, and the list can go on. Over time I have come to notice that ultimately the focus on grooming a child to be a successful adult has lost its place in society. And I believe that fathers are the only ones who can fix this situation. Because the last several decades have shown that everyone who says that they are for children and want what's best for them are liars to some degree.

This may be a guide to some but it's also a reference tool for parents to create successful adults. The other reason for this book is because unfortunately we are solitary individuals who like to clean up our own messes so we never communicate in a formal way to inform each other what is coming ahead in the future. I will do my best to give you enough of a realistic view of the obstacles you will have to face to become the best parent you can be for the betterment of your children. I will not be pulling any punches or waste any time. Let's get right to it.

My First Lesson

When I was 25 I got a call from a judge about verifying my identity. This was a child support hearing to make sure I was an adult so my Father could cease his payments. They told him to pay $1,000 and be done. Mind you I never got the money though. For years I had been at odds with my father over him not "taking care of me." Then at 25 I was over that because years prior when I was a senior in college I was basically homeless and working to pay my way through school. I got a call from my grandmother telling me to use the child support money that my dad had been paying while I was in college. I had no idea what she was talking about. At that moment I called my mother and confronted her about the money. She told me "It's my money! I earned it!" and hung up. Needless to say we didn't speak for years. My father was not a perfect man but at that moment not only did I realize my view of him was skewed, I also had to look back on the truth that he spoke that I didn't listen to. You see, not only had I lost out on money to get me from living out of my car. More importantly I lost over a decade of a relationship because I blindly took one side and ignored another. But in that moment I learned a valuable lesson. Kids need proof. I went backtracking stories and situations in my head. As I got older I went fishing through records because in that situation I had lost both of my parents. No one was to be trusted because my whole idea of trust was completely shattered and I was the only one who had to deal with it being put back together.

Here's the most disturbing thing though. When I was in college this was the reality for a good number of students. Some think it's the homesick freshman, sheltered child, or the college isn't for me kid that has trouble or drops out. They forget about the kids with family problems that explode when the child reaches the age of legal adulthood and that last child support payment goes through. So many deal with the reality of feeling used, thrown away, or flat out turned on by one or both parents due to the constant battle that the child's well-being gets lost in. Also finding out that their Dad wasn't there biological dad as adults. As well as fellow classmates thinking that they sired children that DNA testing proved otherwise. So first and foremost get a DNA test to be sure. Technology is a perfect resolution to that because they don't have to go back and forth about speculation and by whatever age they are mature enough to handle it. They can see that you have seen them as a priority for a long time and cared enough to protect their mental well-being. Because we as adults can see the other adults who still have mommy and daddy issues that will never be resolved because there is no proof.

Contents

Introduction – 2

My First Lesson – 4

Table of Contents – 6

Lessons

A Nation Of Alienation– 8

Always Have A Plan – 12

Be Your Best You – 16

Build A Foundation – 20

Culture Shock Therapy – 23

Dating And Moving On – 26

Dealing With Families And Spouses – 29

Get Organized – 34

Gold Over Glitter – 39

Happy And Healthy – 41

It Won't Be Fair – 47

It's Game Time – 50

Know Who You Are Dealing With – 53

Let It All Play Out – 57

Live Beneath Your Means – 60

Make Lots Of Lemonade – 66

Moving Parts – 69

Parenting Forward – 73

Plant The Principles – 79

Stay The Course – 84

Teach Them How To Fish – 87

Technology Is Your Best Friend – 91

The Adult Judgement – 99

The Emotional Rollercoaster – 103

The Legal System – 110

Time Flies – 116

Tough Love Is Still Love – 121

Understanding Abuse And Addiction – 126

Unorthodox Parenting – 129

Using And Becoming Wise Counsel – 132

A Nation of Alienation

Parental alienation has become a part of the normal dealings of the realm of co-parenting. Families have become accustomed to the time and access issues that go with this topic. Spouses have become accustomed to the physical, mental, and emotional strain that this issue presents their significant others. Law enforcement has begun to recognize the nuances that come with this issue. The educational system has been dealing with the wavering emotions of the children in the circumstances. Counselors and therapists have begun to see a more holistic view of the big picture. Society has also been able to decipher the differences between custodial and noncustodial parents.

When dealing with the family aspect, you have a side that has majority of the access and a side that lacks access. Some children look at it as they have two separate families and some children look at it as if their family is the one that they are with the majority of the time. Depending on the situation you may have the child's complete family having no problem with building a relationship with the child. Then again you may have a family who can be completely blocked out of a child's life. As an example, you and your family may be blocked from calling and social media. And you can see both dynamics within the same family with different children. Which in some ways creates unnecessary tension for the child to deal with. Because one child may enjoy all of the benefits of both sides of the family while being related to another family member relegated to just one side. This is normally when children start asking questions that adults don't want to answer.

The same process goes with dealing with spouses. You know you don't get to approve or disapprove of your ex's choice in mates. That does not mean that the spouse doesn't get to form their own opinion of the other parent. It can range from them seeing that the other parent is uninvolved by their own actions. To them seeing that the other parent is uninvolved due to their significant others actions. The variety of interactions and responses is ultimately dependent on the type of person that spouse is. Some of these things will play out in blending a family. Even though these relationships will affect the children involved in them. It more so is a way for the adults to show their level of maturity and integrity.

Domestic disputes used to be looked at as a one-sided cut and dry situation. Over time that has changed. Even if the procedure is still the same as it once was the ability to read between the lines has definitely been enhanced. Even people within law enforcement have had to deal with the fair and unfair aspects of parental alienation within their own departments with their coworkers. The humiliation of getting detained for no reason has also happened to officers of the law. The unnecessary interfering in someone's parenting time is well documented. The miscarriage of justice directed to parents doing the right thing has been deemed morally unfair for a long period of time. But like I said before, that doesn't mean the laws have changed.

Neither does it mean the ability to enforce them has either. But it has brought in the idea of discretion.

In regards to schools. Teachers, counselors, and therapists have all found themselves looking at these situations differently. Even though schools had a history of being rude to noncustodial parents. They are evolving out of generalizing people that they haven't met or talked to as villainous entities. More teachers are open to having conversations with both parents separately. More counselors are open to children talking to the noncustodial parent more often. Therapists also realize that parent and client confidentiality is for both parents in regards to the child. Also because this facilitates a happy child. And a happy child is a happy student. Due to the fact that there have been too many unhappy children acting out their frustrations during the time that they were supposed to be getting an education. Add to that the growing trend of teachers engaging in sexual misconduct with students. I would assume that parental alienation is one of the factors that creates the opportunity to take advantage of the child. In regards to therapy and other diagnoses I'm pretty sure that if a child needs therapy because of their "noncustodial" parent it's going to send a red flag to the therapists about the custodial home also. But this is still a problem because of the over medicating of children. There are still parents and doctors who will diagnose, prescribe, and drug children without the other parent's knowledge. And will even continue if the parent got a second opinion to the contrary. Some do it for money, some do it for control. Either way it's common knowledge that people do these things.

In this common knowledge is where society steps in. Because people deal with these scenarios with their families, friends, and coworkers. They also begin to see the patterns. They also know the nuances and see the back-and-forth between the parents and the child. It is also figured out who is right and who is wrong. Nobody is 100% right, but at this point people are quite comfortable gauging the percentages. So in some instances people will give other people help. Yet in other instances people will avoid you like the plague. In a nutshell, society will balance out the credit and karma to both parents and families on the right or wrong side of parental alienation.

Always have a plan.

"Train a child in the way that you would want them to go." This is a phrase that we've probably heard in religious terms for our entire lives. So simply put have a plan for your child. The analysis of right and wrong comes into play. Manners, morals, work ethic, and most importantly cause-and-effect. If you don't give your child direction who will? Teachers will come and go until they graduate college. We as parents will be the only yearly constant. So take advantage of the interactions and the ability to formulate new strategies to build a successful child. Now this doesn't mean that they will agree with your plans. What it does mean is they have some kind of set direction and a way of knowing how to complete a task. For example, you may want them to read at a level that may be ahead of all of their age group. That would involve you reading and comprehending with the child. There are plenty of books that you can pick up that will fit their interest to hold their attention. So it will be a win-win situation. You get the child away from TV and frivolous entertainment on to sparking their imagination with reading and improving their reading ability at the same time. They may not know that they are ahead of their peers by the time they're done or by the time to put the plan is successful. But what will be evident is the completion of the phenomenal plan.

We do these type of things all the time. This is how coaches coach up teams to be successful. They have a certain system or a winning formula and each year they repeat and tailor it to the talent on their new team. So take advantage of being the John Wooden of your child's life. One of the best things to look at is your personal successes and failures. Within the confines of your experiences you will be able to find lessons that you can teach to your child that will progress their intellect beyond the level of their peers. You see when you pass down a plan you pass down knowledge. And that knowledge and planning in principle alone can be a stairway to success. So just like any coach, start your plan off with mastering the fundamentals. Once you've got the basics out of the way, take it to the next level. The plan isn't to build a certain type of child, it is merely a way to challenge them to grow and evolve while gaining self-confidence. This is why I use the coaching reference. Most sports have interchangeable motions, that in different sports work to the athletes benefit. Take for example a cornerback or safety may learn how to judge a ball by playing baseball in the outfield. Now they may not have the same passion for one sport as they do the other, but they do take the benefits of that from that one sport into the other.

Some may want their child to be a mechanic but they have a passion to be a carpenter. There are certain fundamentals of buildings that are interchangeable in that scenario. So take advantage of the opportunity to lay a foundation that will build the child into a successful adult by implementing your plan for their positive growth. The beauty of this is the options are all yours and based upon your knowledge, experience, and ingenuity. Another great thing about this is you along with your plan will have to be flexible. Not only creating a better way to learn with a child if necessary but also teaching them how to adapt and adjust to thrive in any scenario. Which leads you to ask a yourself a few questions.

- What do I want my child to be?
- What does my child want to be?
- What does it take to be successful at it?
- What is the best plan of action?
- How can we mesh both plans together?
- Who is the best team for the job?
- What is the degree of difficulty?
- What is the level of passion for the dream?
- What are the rewards and consequences?

Now understand that your plan will be changeable. The only consistent thing about it may be that it is inconsistent. Because at some point your child may want to apply your plan for them for something that is more interesting to them. Which is perfectly fine. Your plan is simply the foundation for them to have a direction. When they find their own direction use your wisdom and intellect to produce the best results with your years of experience in planning and successfully mastermind your child's evolution into adulthood. Which, by the way also pays it forward. Because it is that type of interaction that a child becomes an adult from, which will enable them to teach their children how to become adults too. That is the beauty of a great plan. One of the simplest and most effective ways to teach your child how to strategize is to sit down at a table and teach them how to play chess. It shows if they can plan ahead, plan for the oppositions attack and retreat. So once they get the idea cemented in their brain to be two or three steps ahead of their competition they will be able to formulate their own plans and come back to you as wise counsel.

Having a plan also is paramount for dealing with the social environment that will surround the rearing of your child. There is a point where you want to know what's effective and what's ineffective with the people that you dealing with. And with the experience of knowing who is reliable and unreliable or who will be the best suited support system member to facilitate the best results for your child in situational experiences is necessary and also teachable. Not only will you be teaching self-sufficiency with planning, but the effects of teamwork and networking. Simply put, no success was ever done alone. The same also goes for future planning like college, trade school, business starting, investing, family and estate planning, and normal childhood wants. Remember when we were kids they would say "Santa Claus knows which kids are naughty or nice." So in order to get the gifts we wanted, we had to plan to be on your best behavior. Thus the ultimate goal is to have a plan that you can implement that will make your child be in the habit of planning for success, setting goals, following through, and achieving each objective.

Become The Best You

The gravity of this particular type of pressure in life can test anyone's intestinal fortitude. But the same type of pressure can create a reinvigorated and focused parent. You can't control other people's ideas or ideologies but what you can control is yourself and your effort. The best you that you wanted to be is still within you and can be carved and sculpted by you. There is no limitation to proving yourself right. With only one life to live, why not be the best of whatever it is that you set your mind to be. Before you can do this for your child do this for yourself. If you are happy with who you are, then it is perfectly okay to improve on that. If you are unhappy with who you are is perfectly okay for you to make that change. If you have to find peace, then find it. If you have to find a passion take that journey. If you have to find motivation find that catalyst. Because when you find yourself and you find your purpose you will most certainly find life.

The reality of life is we are all special and we all have greatness within us. Maybe before you can believe it you may need to accept it. You are great at something! You are here for reason! There is no one like you and there will never be! Your individuality is one of your greatest gifts in life. Use it! I know that parental alienation does a number on a human being. It's a constant pain of not being able to share the greatest things within you that you will freely give to the greatest thing you've ever created. Yes, your time may be limited and your obstacles may be unfair and insulting. But that doesn't mean you can't be the best you in that limited time or through those ridiculous obstacles. Make those times timeless because nothing in life is promised or guaranteed. When you find that passion for something it will create a chain reaction that your child will find a passion for something. Also it can either inspire them to live a certain life and/or give them a reference point to take what's most useful from their parents lives and apply it to their own. There you will have common some ground. An understanding about the joy of waking up in the morning to do something you love and to be something that you want to be.

Of course there will be bumps in the road, but the journey never stops for a few bumps. So you just keep on trucking. You may have a vision but you don't have a plan. Will yourself into figuring it out as you go. It's okay to make mistakes because there are lessons to be learned. You don't embark on a new journey and know exactly where each road leads. What you will eventually become will have an element of trial and error to it. Don't let it define you. The Family Court system may have left you depressed or broken. Remember, they are only inside of a building and cannot define you in the world. People may tell you no a million times but they don't get a say in the life you are trying to build. To you some things may seem impossible but to some impossible is just a word that means you haven't done it yet. I don't care where it starts. If you commit to weight loss you will see results. If you commit to personal growth you will evolve. If you commit to being the best parent you can be, you will become it. If you commit to greatness you will become great. So the only thing you have to do is commit. And no one can dictate that to you and no one can take that away from you.

We all have heroes that we look up to. Those heroes come in all shapes and sizes. They come from all different backgrounds and a lot of different circumstances. Yet they all have a few things in common. One of those things is that their passion was able to meet with opportunity. You'll know when an opportunity will present itself, but that doesn't matter if you are not sincere to your passion. If your passion is your child be sincere to it. If you feel you're going up against a brick wall get a rock hammer and be Andy Dufresne. Time does not matter, people's opinions do not matter, your goal is the only thing that matters. Because that goal and the pursuit of it is when life begins and where life becomes everlasting. You want to be able to hear your kids and grandkids say your name with a sense of pride. Your journey to become the best you will give them the confidence to know that the best is in their blood.

Ultimately, when you do this do this for you because you are the first person you will wake up to tomorrow morning. You are who's always staring at you in the mirror. Your battle within is the one that you are in complete control to be the victor of. When you are up make it a blowout and when you're down you can make a comeback. Life is completely what you make it. You will have to look fear in the eyes.

You will have to destroy your comfort zone. You will have to work like you've never worked before. You will have to face your own demons. You will have to stand up unapologetically in yourself. And you will have to accept the valleys and peaks along the journey. When you can look at you with pride and humility everyone around you will begin to understand why. There is no shame in falling and getting up. There is no shame from learning a lesson and becoming a teacher. So there would definitely be no shame in you searching within to find the best you and bringing it out. Remember along the way that joy and pain are twins just like greatness and mediocrity. You see the one thing that parents cannot give children is effort but you can give it to yourself and let it spread to the people around you.

Build A Foundation

Most people have heard the parable of the man who built his home on the side of a mountain versus the man who built his home in sand. This pretty much goes the same for parenting. If you don't build upon a solid foundation, the home you built is destined to crumble. Within this parable a few things are present. Intelligence, foresight, and work ethic to name a few. These are some of the things that will probably have to be taken into consideration when you're building a foundation.

Be a thinker. Once you come up with a plan, come up with the scenarios that would test the theory of your plan. If you build a relationship on trust it is easier to decipher fact from fiction. If you build a relationship on lies. You don't know which fact or which fiction is the one that will ultimately cause that structure to fall. So my opinion is it's best to be honest when building the foundation with your child. This can start with using Santa Claus is an example. In the beginning you say that Santa Claus only gives gifts to the nice kids. As a child gets older someone informs them that Santa Claus isn't real. It is at that moment that jolly old St. Nick is no longer able to be the scapegoat for the presents that you "didn't" buy. For some it was easy to throw Santa under the bus. For others Santa Claus was not about to take credit for the effort and love that was put into creating a great Christmas. Now some of us grow out of it and others re-create the process when we are creating new memories with a new child.

Also, for some of us the seasonal festivities are a moment to teach the principles that the holiday season is really meant to embody. Though it may seem like a childish analogy the meat of the metaphor's this. Some of us embody the spectacle and fake the substance and others embody the substance and fake the spectacle.

Use your foresight. In order to use it effectively you have to trust in the systems that you are educated in. You see a silo was created from someone's past mistake of not preparing for drought or surplus. As a parent you have to have a plan for when things go good and when things go bad. You know the oldest lesson in the world is teaching people why they shouldn't touch a hot stove. To the point now it's innately a reaction because the closer your hand is the fire the more your brain tells you to back off. Conversely when doing something positive you get the feeling of confidence to keep going. This is where foresight is important because there is a lesson of balance within it. That is, too much of something is a bad thing and too little of something is a bad thing. So you have to make sure your child is at an even keel, never too high never too low. The reason is foresight prepares you for extremes but also doesn't let you live in them. Because when you teach a child not to touch a hot stove but you don't tell them to cut off the gas because you need the fire to cook. Just like the balance in the silo. You can use the surplus to feed your hunger or use your surplus to increase your wealth. But you have to give them the ability to see both angles.

Without work there is no reward. The difference between the two foundations and their subsequent success or failure involved the work that it took to create them. It took a far greater amount of time and effort to chisel a foundation on the side of a rock than it did to dig a hole in some sand. Though ultimately they both built themselves a home. One was built to last, and the other was built for obsolescence. So as the old saying goes "The best things in life are worth working hard for". First you crawl, then you walk, then you run, then you bike, then you drive, and then you fly. Because if you didn't follow the process you would only know how to crawl and fly with no concept of speed and landing. Sometimes the difficult thing is not succumbing to taking shortcuts. Because the house that washed away could have been a magnificent structure, but the shortcut it was built upon created a beautiful disaster. If you're able to cultivate a respect for effort it will only heighten the understanding of foresight and intelligence. Which enables you to have the ability to take your time to create a masterpiece and improve upon it even while withstanding the elements.

Culture Shock Therapy

When dealing with children it is wise to show them different perspectives and cultures. That way they begin to understand that different people do things the same or differently. When it comes to principles and virtues most of us have the same model. But when it comes to other things such as cooking, dancing, religion, and regional lifestyles things begin to become more diverse. You may speak different languages and have different customs that can teach your child a completely different level of respect for themselves and for other people. So let's get into some ways to shake things up a bit.

Cooking is one of the foundations of family but people cook differently. They're different specialties that are present on the north, south, east, and west. Some of these specialties even deal with the same exact type of dish. There is American food, which has its different subcultures as well as Asians and Hispanics. You can use the things that you've learned and fuse them with different cultures to create an atmosphere of learning through food. You may not have thought to put jerk chicken with Lo Mein noodles or in taco's. But your child may like the taste of them all. So a gateway into understanding another culture is through using some of the things that your child may like to eat. Which will lead them into having a deeper interest for other aspects of their culture that they may find appealing. It helps to broaden a child's horizons.

The same goes for dancing and other activities. When children are babies if you throw on some music they began to bounce. We've all gathered around to see a little child show us their best move when a song comes on. So why not use that natural fun moment as a springboard for growth. It may be something about ballet that catches your child's attention or maybe something about breakdance. Either way it's an activity outside of school that they can learn to express themselves in a natural way that they gravitate to. The same goes for sports and other extracurricular activities such as chess club. Each of these cultures have their own code of conduct and built-in system of competition. They teach the importance of work ethic, preparation, effort, and grace in the event you win or lose. So without having to hands-on teach this you can let their interests teach them that life experience.

Religion for some is a touchy subject because some people react differently to different religions. But religion itself teaches a belief system and the principles of right and wrong within their belief system. You may have two people of two different religions who were able to interact and coexist cohesively because they understand the principles of right and wrong. So if you're Christian and someone's Muslim that doesn't make you mortal enemies. All it does is give you different perspectives on certain aspects of spirituality. And at some point your child is going to ask what's the difference between this type of person and that type of person? People may dress differently, maybe worship on different days, but the belief is still in a higher power or maybe not at all. Either way it teaches them to respect people's differences because they are not less valid and it doesn't make them less of a person. We all can make it to the same point in different ways.

As far as discipline and structure goes boot camps and etiquette schools are a good option. You will find yourself beating a dead horse when you repeat how things operate in your household over and over again. Well by putting your child in this different type of environment it will definitely give them a culture shock that says things in the real world work off of the principles in the home. Boot camp doesn't allow you just keep your room messy and neither does etiquette school. It doesn't allow you the opportunity to be insubordinate. So by placing them in this environment they will begin to see hands-on that in life there is a reason for structure. Some kids who go a little too far may need to be in a scared straight program. The thing about these programs is to show them a glimpse of the reality that is ahead of them opposed to the fantasy that they have in their mind. This also goes for the other aspects of culture shock. When the world that you live in is not defined by unrealistic stereotypes but instead by realistic life experiences your child will be better equipped to navigate this big world that we live in.

Dating and Moving On

All things good or bad must come to an end. This is also true for dating and moving on. It's also a problem for some who don't date and don't move on. There are instances in life where two people go their separate ways and come back together. And there are instances in life where two people grow apart. That doesn't mean that that was the only person that will ever be for you. At some point you either have to learn to or gradually let go. Once you let go you may need some time to decompress and get back to the best you. In that paradigm you may have some period of time to break down your own walls and let down your guards. Unfortunately, the emotional roller coaster can leave a bad taste in your mouth when it pertains to the opposite sex. But at some point we have to be realistic, bitterness will only increase loneliness.

Rule number one. <u>Do not go back to your ex</u>. There is no reason to rebuild a bad relationship under the same terms that made it bad. This means, no sex because you are comfortable with them. This means, no dating them because you're uncomfortable meeting new people. This means, no sabotaging the interactions with the new people you meet to find a way back to your ex. This means, no vying for their attention whether it be in a positive or negative way. This ultimately means, drop your baggage and keep the lesson.

Rule number two. <u>Do not make any hasty decisions</u>. Sometimes people have knee-jerk reactions as a quick fix. When you move on it, it's understandable that you may be embarking on a new journey. That doesn't necessarily mean you turn into a completely different person overnight. This means, don't introduce new people into the parental relationship until it is right. This means, don't find yourself under someone new when you're not over someone old. This means, you can't find yourself by continually creating a new self. This means, you cannot make decisions out of spite. This means, you do not create a new persona that is a replacement for you the person. This also means, you do not make big financial decisions i.e. homes, cars, shopping sprees, vacations, and other frivolous activities to occupy your time instead of dealing with the reality.

Rule number three. <u>Do not make your future pay for the past</u>. What happened in the past and who it happened with doesn't give you a free pass to take it out on the world. This means, you do not insult people and disrespect people that you don't know. This means, you do not invite people into your space so they can be a punching bag. This means, you don't have entitlement issues with strangers. This means, the new world does not owe you with the old world does. This means, you are expected to act like an adult even when you're in pain. In doing so you will see that other people are able to function just like you will be able to.

Rule number four. <u>Don't be afraid to open new doors</u>. For every door in life that closes another one opens. Do not let your past disappointments shackle you from your future opportunities. That's the beauty of embarking on a journey. This means, do not curse yourself with your own mouth. This means, do not enter into things expecting to be disappointed. This means, commit to doing something all the way instead of looking for a justification to bailout. This means opening up to new possibilities from the new vantage point to see life differently. This means, take the bull by the horns and don't pass the buck.

Rule number five. <u>Learn from your past mistakes</u>. One of the magnificent beauties about failure is it allows you to have a lesson to learn from. Once you learn the lesson you can improve on that lesson without making the same mistakes. This means, you take an honest evaluation of the mistakes you made. This means, you atone those mistakes by changing the pattern that created them. This means, you walk the walk. This means, you become better to yourself, to your child, and your future partner. Honestly if you do not learn from your mistakes you will be doomed to repeat them. So why not just graduate to better things. Because it is better to live a good life than a good lie.

Dealing With Families And Spouses

Along with dealing with co-parenting you will be dealing with co-families. Between the two families you may have a different ideology when it comes to parenting itself. There may be a relationship that is respectful and focused on your child's development. Then again there may be a relationship that is disrespectful and not focused on your child's development. Either way you are the parent you have to deal with this. So at some point you either make the situation better or make it worse. The same goes for dealing with new spouses. Some people are a pleasure to have around your children and other people you may feel the need to watch very closely. But along the way there are a few guidelines to follow that will keep the peace.

Whether you have a good relationship or bad relationship with the family there needs to be a certain level of respect. If your child loves them, then you have to respect that they are doing something right. If you don't see any fault or malice in the situation from your vantage point even if there's bad blood you might as well let the past be the past. That doesn't mean you don't keep your radar up. It just means you don't have to fish for a problem that isn't there. Being cordial at the least creates a healthy relationship. There will be times where you will be needed because of your DNA. Your child will act in ways that they are not accustomed to just by nature alone. So when those things happen they're going to need your perspective and advice. In order to get there the lines of communication have to be open. For others it's a bit more difficult. Some families are difficult to deal with because of the enjoyment they get out of playing games using the child. In this scenario, if you don't have anything nice to say don't say anything at all. The reason for this is because if you have a disagreement, the possibility of them taking it out on your child and alienating you from your child to find out what's going on is high. No matter where you are your primary concern is safety. Once that is established everything else can fall into play.

Dealing with spouses is a bit similar but a bit tricky. It can range from people who you don't even know exist to people who you are comfortable enough with to involve them in the co-parenting. Starting with people who don't exist. This can also go both ways because there are some people who are respectful to both parents and do not want to get involved and there are other people who were told not to get involved so they are hidden. Either way the bottom line is you need to know who's around your child. That doesn't mean you get to approve or disapprove who your ex is dating. Rather approve or disapprove the parameters in which they will be able to involve themselves with your child. If they're the type of person who is willing to have a conversation or is probably a parent an understanding is easier. If they are the type of person, who is not willing to have any communication then they may not be around for a significant amount of time anyway or they're going to be a problem. Everything really starts with that conversation just to feel out the other person and let them know where you stand. If it doesn't happen due to the other parent it is pretty much a high chance that it will affect their relationship because it's dysfunctional.

These same family and spouse rules apply for yourself also. Under that mantra it takes a village, and you have to give access to the village. That doesn't mean you get to dictate the interaction with your family and spouse in a negative way. Because what if you are not available at a particular point but your family side of the equation is still needed. Someone has to be there who is able to be neutral and focus on what's most important. So numbers, addresses, emails, and other contact information is imperative. The child may not always be with you or the other parent so you have to know other people's contact information. They may be spending the night somewhere or at a birthday party with a different family member or spouse. It happens, it's part of the process so you will have to deal with it. But, the same level of respect goes both ways also. If they don't have anything nice to say, advise them to say nothing at all. Due to the fact that people use these lines of communication between family, friends, and spouses as a way to fish for information. These type of tactics only create a worse situation because when trying to extend the trust someone may sabotage and destroy it.

You will be able to gauge the level of safety or danger when communicating with the child. If there always bubbly and happy then you know they feel comfortable. If they are always tense and apprehensive, then you know something is wrong. When they have a conversation with you without interruption and correction you're communicating in a good space. If there's always congestion and confusion about what to say to you then it's probably because they're watching your child talk because they want to hide something. But you'll be able to gauge by the energy itself, it's undeniable. Also families and spouses can be your greatest asset or your greatest obstacle. Due to the fact that you have to get to the bottom of the family and spouses intentions in regards to your child. There are some who know they are part of a team to create a productive member of society. And there are others who are opportunistic and use these situations for their own diabolical game. You will easily know the difference. With one, your child will be helped to figure out the best direction to go on their journey. With the other, your child will be used to take a journey that leads nowhere. Either way remember your hands are never really tied that's just an illusion.

As far as feeling like your hands are tied. Make it clear early on that if you have to show up to right the ship wherever the ship may be, you will. Just make sure you do that correctly. By that I mean let people know you are coming. Don't just show up unannounced! If you have to record it or call the police in advance to meet you somewhere do that. Some people will respect it and some people will try to play games to get you in a negative situation. Either way they know that they will have to deal with you over the telephone or in person. The reason for that is that some people in worst-case scenarios will band together to cover up abuse. That is not only detrimental but probably unforgivable for most. Most noncustodial parents know this to be true because when serious things happen they may go a short or long time period without being able to communicate with their child. This usually lasts until whatever situation has gone wrong blows over. To be more specific using the opposite side of the spectrum. When everybody knows times, dates of events, and all the important details. Then there is a sense of trust and camaraderie for what's in the best interest of the child. When you constantly have to go outside of the family and friend dynamic team to get information i.e. report cards to medical information. You know quickly that there is a serious, serious problem. In order to keep this problem at a minimum always be personable. Be consistent about being open even if you feel that the people you're communicating with aren't completely open or personable with you. If you do that you either build a bridge of communication or be able to feel the energy of the weight of the lie that is trying to be told to you. Either way, be prepared for that and everything in between.

Get Organized

Two things that every child needs, is structure and discipline. In order to effectively give that you have to have a structured and disciplined life yourself. There is no way to teach these things by rhetoric. So in order to show why it is important you must actively organize yourself in a way that maximizes your productivity. See kids have a different way of operating when they know their own schedule. Sometimes parents will overschedule because they don't get the time that they feel is necessary to make a significant impact on development. But I'm here to tell you that you don't have to do that. Reason being is because structure allows you to make a schedule that can involve multiple activities that are not only fun but also necessary for development.

For instance, there are small things you can do that save time in teaching children how to save time. There also big things you can do that take up time but is also educational. Let us start with small things. You need to have a wake-up time and a bed time. Most people who don't, create an unorganized free for all every morning and every night. So some simple things to do is tell you child to take their bath and put out the clothes for the next day before their bedtime. Also put their dirty clothes in a hamper. It may seem small but trust me it's at timesaver because all they have to do in the morning is put on their clothes. So this gives them more time to make their beds, brushed their teeth, comb their hair, and eat breakfast.

Also it keeps to the school regimen and works effectively even during summer time and breaks from school. But in order to drive this home completely you have to be doing it too. Because if you get up and are organized and ready go at a certain time they have no choice but to be on the same page.

When it comes to household chores inside or outside of the home you have to maintain that efficiency. You absolutely have to give your child chores to do. But when it pertains to cleanliness create an atmosphere where there is never a big mess to clean up after in the first place. If you, pick up after yourself they will begin to pick up after themselves. Sometimes when children go between households they will continue to do what they have been doing at one home because it's a habit. If it's positive leave it alone if it's negative it's going to need some work. But if your habit is structure, over time it will begin to be infectious. Because your child can't come to you asking where things are because everything has its designated place. This also goes for the time and place you may put out the trash. The reason I use these small examples is because a child may want to watch television or play games or do what it is they consider fun. You want to teach them a schedule and organizational skills so they will come to find out they have more time to do things they want to do if they maintain a certain amount of order as opposed to creating a mess and spending a whole day procrastinating trying not to fix it.

This also goes for educational purposes. Whether they are in school or out of school there should be a designated time and time amount for enhancing their intelligence. Have a time for reading so you can be able to see their progress. If it's Christmas break, spring break, or summer time buy a workbook and have them work in it, daily to keep sharp. Have them work at least 15 minutes a day on both. Because you as a parent have a job and you as a parent have to let them know that their education is their job. So there will be no fun without the work that precedes it. This organization also creates bonding time because it's a one-on-one teacher student relationship. This also goes for the weekend projects like gardening, home improvements, car maintenance, and other life management skills that involve effort to maintain something.

When it comes to big things like school, daycare, summer camp, extracurricular activities, and events. You keep the consistency of being on time, being prepared for which you need to do that day, dressing for the occasion, and understanding your parameters. Let's use a field trip for an example. Kids love and anticipate that field trip going wherever. They want you to sign the permission slip and tell you what they want to bring for lunch and know what they want to wear. Well in the midst of all of this there is a certain expectation of behavior prior to, during, and after this field trip. If you don't meet the requirements you don't get to go. If you do meet the requirements you get everything you asked for. This same structure is commonly used with extracurricular activities. If you don't have your schoolwork together, you don't get to participate. But once again this is also something you have to do in your day-to-day life as a parent. Be open and able to discipline yourself if you fall off of the wagon. Because structure and discipline has a healthy amount of self-correction.

Speaking of health, you need to have a workout routine and a healthy diet. Reason being is because society is getting heavier and lazier as we speak. So creating an active environment for yourself creates an active environment for your child. If you exercise, then they want to exercise. If you eat healthy, they will eat healthy. And if you see results, they will begin to see results. And of course you both can enjoy a cheat day. But the beauty of that cheat day is you both will be able to appreciate it because you've put in the work to earn it. I don't know what it is but a milkshake tastes better when you have been waiting all week to have it. Now when you first see the benefits of being structured and organized work itself out in your life you will begin to see it only creates more benefits for your child. When you manage your time properly you have more time to do things. When you manage your space properly you have more space to work with. When you organize your thoughts you have a higher probability of completing more tasks. When you maintain your health you have more energy to be able to do more things. And when you structure your money properly you have more money to work with to be able to do more with your child.

"So when you look good you feel good, when you feel good you play good, when you play good they pay good, when they pay good you eat good, when you eat good you live good!" I got that from Deion Sanders and it is so correct.

Gold Over Glitter

In life most people follow The Golden Rules. Rule number one "Treat people the way you want to be treated." and rule number two "He who has the gold makes the rules." Both of these rules work in parenting. In essence you are modeling the behavior that your child will adapt to and eventually re-create as an adult. If you take care of your child when they are young, they would take care of you when you're old. If you use your money wisely you will teach them to use their money wisely. So what I mean by gold over glitter is giving your child the lessons that are timeless currency and not the flash that is a fad for a certain era.

The first gold you can give them is yourself and the first glitter you can give them are frivolous things. Do not ever try to substitute your time for material. There are things that you can teach and moments that you can share that are priceless. So no matter what type of item you may purchase it will never replace that priceless memory. Of course you may use money to help create that moment but there is a difference between investing in a moment and buying love. You are the blueprint of what a parent should be or should not be. So the first thing you should be is available. At some point child is going to call you about something and that is when you're their superhero or the sidekick.

The other gold you give them is truth. Lies may sound good or make someone feel good but they are always just a temporary fix. The look of disappointment that you get when you let someone live a lie is heartbreaking. Don't do it to them and don't do it to yourself. Besides truth has a better return on its investment. It builds bridges, creates discourse, is a major foundation for problem solving, and most importantly cements respect. You won't have to waste the time of qualifying yourself because your word is backed by a gold standard.

One of the most overlooked pieces of gold you can give is humility. It may not seem like much and it is often overlooked but it is a highly valuable substance. Teach them that they don't need to be the center of attention all the time. That there is a regal energy that is connected to being humble. Let them know the reason that "It is better to give than to receive." is because the giver can always produce more to give. People are not going to always like you. My grandparents used to tell me "They hated Jesus too." So the moral of the story is people still speak of Jesus, they don't know of the people who hated him.

Happy and Healthy

Two very essential parts of life are the mental and physical health of an individual. This also goes for your personal life and your parenting life. You can't be your best or give your best when you're not 100%. So you have to create some type of space to maintain being in the best physical and mental condition to be the best person and parent you can be. Good habits just like any other habit will be contagious when people see positive results. So here's why you should be getting into the habit of being the most positive and productive human being possible.

When it pertains to happy, just like your physical health it's going to take constant work to maintain. You're going to have to learn how to be flexible and roll with the punches. Everything that goes on in life should not upset you or get you stressed out. This is not a call to be naïve about the situations life will present but rather carving out a solution from a place of peace. Now this can go on in various different ways. One of those ways is the things that you put into your psyche. Television, movies, music, books, and any other type of artwork visual and audio that can be consumed into the mind. When you gravitate more to comedies you will be open to have a sense of humor about more circumstances. When you gravitate towards drama it may peak your minds sense of skepticism. So in using those small examples be wary of your mental intake because it can come out in your emotional response. A positive person is more likely to be able to take advice and implement the advice than a negative one.

The same goes for this level of positivity when it comes to your relationship which a child. Happy people are fun to be around. That infectious personality that other people gravitate to. Your child will begin to gravitate to you because of it. That doesn't mean you don't teach the lessons of life but what it does mean is that you can handle life and still have a good time. Which by the way can curve your child's responses to negative situations with a more positive outlook. They may be less prone a lash out and throw tantrums when they don't get their way because they've watched you handle life's tough situations with some sort of grace and a smile. Also, it makes the good experiences better due to the fact that you can build upon positivity with more joy. Now in a society where we seem to remember the negative very profoundly people secretly remember all the positive also. Let's be perfectly honest, happy people make the world go around. The confidence that positivity can create is exponentially better when you get to a space where it begins to come from within. I recall once doing an experiment in my psychology class. Part of the experiment was to surround a person and whisper something positive to them about themselves. At the end of this experiment everyone felt more empowered and able to do more things. That sense of confidence didn't wear off in the next couple of hours or days. People carried that energy within for significant period of time. Do the same with yourself in the mirror and with the child and reap the benefits of the positive results.

You see happy people have a certain vigor for life in the works that they do in life. Things become less of a task which doesn't allow for a morbid experience. It becomes fun. Just something as simple as the task of vacuuming the floor is a whole lot more entertaining when you're doing it listening to your favorite song. It makes the time go by and makes the experience more memorable than forgettable. It is that approach that will make every experience that much more fulfilling because that energy will be reciprocated. So it begins the reverse of hurt people hurt people to its nice to be nice.

Now this is the type of approach you need to take to your physical health also. Longevity is rooted in the thought that your health will be an anchor that keeps you steady long enough to fulfill the plans that you have made. So to complete your plans you do have to be a body that stays in motion and eats healthy. We all want to see our kids grow up and have kids. Barring unforeseen circumstances, we all know that exercise and diet are a recipe for longevity in life. That is also a recipe for success which a child can aspire to be at your age. In my family I was taught at a young age that we age gracefully. In that process I was also taught a proper diet and encouraged to do physical activities. As a result of that I am as healthy now as I was 20 years ago. There is nothing I can't do with my child and it sets a precedent for my child to be able to do the same when they become a parent.

My personal confession is that I'm a foodie. But along the way I've learned through various experimentations with cooking foods that I can make that taste good to me and are good for me. Not only are they benefits in my physical aesthetics but also my mental sharpness. Also a proper diet can cleanse the body of toxins which with the increase of medications can help you detox your child. You will see the difference in growth, skin, and hair just to name a few. Another benefit that came about was the ability to cook with my child and pass down recipes that they can use for themselves. Nothing brings together people like a good meal. In this paradigm I was able to not only teach good foods from bad foods, but also how to shop on a budget which is something that came in handy in those college years. The pride and resourcefulness of creating a five-star tasting meal on a one-star budget that will always attract company and conversation. And hopefully those conversations and company will educate you and enlighten you about other aspects of health that you can incorporate into your lifestyle.

Now the physical part of it for some seems more challenging than others. The beauty of it is you have an endless option of things to do that will keep your body in motion. It is the activity that can also be contagious and inspire your child to begin to be a body that stays in motion. One of the coolest things that I've seen is a father and son weight loss journey. Father wanted to lose weight to be able to be more active with his son and inspired his son to the point where he also became active and involved in team sports. The fact that they worked out together and have this competitive but yet oh so cool interaction is beyond special. When you see two people change and take pride in the fact that they are better than they once were, it makes the whole experience worthwhile. It also plants to seed of self-improvement and maintaining a certain level of excellence. One other thing that it builds is the confidence to know that even if you fall down you can get back up and get right back where you were with a little hard work. I must admit one of the most enjoyable days was taking my child to fitness boot camp and watching him persevere because he wanted to beat dear old dad. The kid out did numerous adults that day and on the way home was happily confident in his abilities, a little cocky too though, but nevertheless the personality was great and hilarious. Also it's a way to set goals. Whether it's an ideal weight goal or time goal the idea that you have to self-motivate yourself to get better not only shows up in the physical but mentally too.

I once remember listening to Mike Tyson talk about happy fighters. In a roundabout way he said they were the most dangerous because they enjoyed the work. They were happy to take instructions to become better and they will also happily take the punishment from life or the opponent to become better. An angry fighter is more rigid and possibly has lost the passion which causes them to look for the easy knockout that may not ever present itself. I bring that up to say that life is a fight. So make the decision to be the happy fighter and you can bring home the championship of the world, while also being able to enjoy the journey. And most importantly be able to create a lifestyle through your joy that can be happily duplicated by all of the people that surround you. Which will have you living that experiment with people surrounding you telling you positive things about yourself that will empower you and encourage you to do more and do a better.

It Won't Be Fair

There are circumstances in life that will not be fair, consider this one of them. If you were able to come to this realization it will be easy to deal with the reality moving forward. Living in the ideology of what should be right and what should be wrong only creates a recipe for frustration. So since life isn't perfect you shouldn't expect it to be perfect for you. I'm not saying expect the worst but I am saying prepare for the worst. Because if you prepare yourself for the worst-case scenario you will have a plan and be able to deal with any other scenario that can be present. In this situation you are the proverbial underdog so don't expect to get the breaks that other people get.

What I mean by that is this. If you are father, you already know how the legal system sees you and treats you statistically. If you are mother, you also know how the system sees you and treats you statistically. There are built-in advantages and disadvantages to both in outcome. This same goes with the dealings with society outside of the legal realm. The way people view parenting and treat parents in public is completely different then the legal process because most of society understands the nuances and are able to read between the lines better. So once again there are certain advantages and disadvantages. Nonetheless a job still has to be done. And that job is to be the best parent you can be under whatever circumstance is presented.

The most important thing about excepting the fairness or unfairness of the process is that it's also unfair to your child too. You have to be able to take a step back and realize that you can work out your emotional issues better than your child can because you're an adult. You won't cry when you're hungry or need attention. You probably won't throw a tantrum when you don't get your way. You see your child will be following your example not setting it. So in these common outcomes you may have to be the first teacher of grace and dignity when being dealt a bad hand. You see if you don't cry over spilled milk then they won't cry over it either. They will clean up the mess and get a new cup just like you. Which is a pretty good quality to teach and it doesn't rob them of their childhood. So once again you become able to accept the reality and make the best of it.

Another aspect of this is that nothing lasts forever. Everything in life is temporary even life itself. So you have to keep that in mind with every decision that you make or that is made for you. It's unfair if you get lied on but no lie can live forever. It's unfair that you may get alienated but children will more often times than not seek out their parents. It's unfair that so much time can be wasted out of spite but when children become parents they also get a different understanding of parenting through their life experiences. So the way they feel at five is different from 10, different from 15, different from 20, different from 30, and so on so forth. That is part that's forgotten of dealing with unfairness. When you're constantly fighting an uphill battle at some point the battle will come to an end. Also, the playing field will be leveled and at that point the rest of your battle will be downhill.

Understand this is easier said than done. But the ability to do it is easier if in the fact you understand upfront that this process will not be fair. There is a certain level of weight that is constantly on someone who is living a lie. That also translates to people living off of the benefits of unfairness. No one gets away a winner or scot-free because if the child's best interest is not a true priority of the parents then someone is taking a hand in a robbing a child of a complete childhood. Though it is not a crime in the court of law it's definitely a crime of parenting, life, and karma. Think about the people you've seen who have benefited off of someone else's pain. They seem to go from celebratory to self-destructive over time. I'm explaining this not to say take solace in another person's suffering behind closed doors. I am merely explaining that there is a reason behind me reiterating do what's in the best interest of the child. It is because they will suffer from the unfairness on both sides of the parenting dynamic. While longing for the connection with the absence of one parent they will be present to watch the self-destruction of another. So with this weight of two adults resting squarely on the shoulders of a child you have to be aware and present that the weight is there in the first place.

It's Game Time

Here's a list of games that may be played.

Legal

- Created arguments to call the police.
- Stalling for time when involved in the custody battle.
- Moving to a different city or state after judgment.
- Petition to get you to pay legal fees and run up the bill.
- Ask for child support increases if you get married.
- Try to contact your lawyer for sympathy.
- Have a lawyer that's constantly unavailable.
- Petition for back child support after already receiving undocumented money.
- Getting a bogus restraining order to hamper your visitation.
- Falsely accusing you of a crime.
- Using the police as a weapon during visitation.
- Use accusations or setups to create supervised visitation.

Parenting

- Undermining the influence of one parent.
- Encouraging your child to be disrespectful or dismissive to you.
- Try to oversee every interaction.
- Attempt to marginalize your contributions in your child's life.
- Over involve one side of the family and alienate the other.
- Create bad behaviors and scapegoat the other parent for trying to correct them.
- Lying about the child's schedule so you miss events.
- Trying to unnecessarily replace one parent with a significant other.
- Making sure child is unavailable to the other parent.
- Using other people as a buffer or bodyguard unnecessarily to create conflict.
- Portraying a parent as abusive for normal parenting.
- Cultivating unnecessary tension between parent and child.

Relationships

- Using a relationship to alienate the other parent.
- Using the child to gain access to a relationship.
- Letting a significant other make parenting decisions without involving both parents.
- Letting a significant other babysit that the other parent has never met.
- Giving a spouse unfettered access to the child while denying the parent access.
- Having a secret relationship with someone who may be unfavorable.
- Having a revolving door of relationships that try to replace the other parent.
- Using a significant other is a go-between to get to the child.
- The significant other believing that they take precedent over another parent.
- Unnecessarily creating "family events" on your parenting time.
- Creating a parenting competition between parent and spouse.
- Creating unnecessary tension in blended families by treating kids differently.

Family

- Speaking negatively on the other side of the family.
- Limiting the access to the other side of the family.
- Creating an atmosphere that encourages loving one side and using the other.
- Not being honest about where a child may get certain characteristics from.
- Demonizing certain characteristics prevalent on the other side of the family.
- Alienation to the point where family become strangers.
- Using family as a "hide out" in order to aid alienation.
- Using family to be gatekeepers for access to your own child.
- Undermining common family values for positioning.
- Introducing friends as family in order to replace the other side of

the family.

- Withholding information because it's "family business" that involves your child.
- Using the family's network and connections to alienate and cause animosity.

Financial

- Use money meant for the child and spend it on other frivolous items.
- Using government assistance along with child support to maintain a lifestyle.
- Consistently being unable to fund extracurricular activities.
- Spending money meant for one child on another.
- Constantly purchasing new items because they are being shared with siblings or family members.
- Paying the other parent for access to the child.
- Paying real or imaginary bills in the other household in order to keep normalcy.
- Using the child as a spy for the purpose of increasing child support.
- Paying the other parent's travel expenses if you live in different areas.
- Using the child as a pawn to collect funds from the extended family.
- Creating conflict and confusion to get out of paying for something.
- Creating overly inflated bills for the other parent to pay out of spite.

Now of course I left out other games that people play. This could be considered the tip of the iceberg. What's important about some of the games I have stated is giving you a framework so you can be able to recognize the games. You can either engage in the games or acknowledge them and decide not to participate.

Know Who You Are Dealing With

There's an old saying that goes "You can catch more flies with honey than with vinegar." That saying is true because we had to study flies. So using the same logic, you should be able to catch more. In order to understand something, you have to study it thoroughly. Once you understand a creature's nature and hunting habits you begin to understand how to approach it. You begin to play to your strengths and its weaknesses in order to accomplish whatever goal is set. You have to understand the different advantages of territory and weather in order to figure out your best plan of action and its probability of success.

So first and foremost you need to know who you are. You have to confront your own strengths and weaknesses. Know your own limitations and how you operate in different circumstances in order to know how to deal with everyone else. Mastery and understanding of self should be your first priority. Being able to operate with a clear mind is immensely important. When you play to your strengths you have less mental and physical restraints to confine you. When you're operating in your weaknesses you need understand your breaking point and what it takes to get you there. Once you have accepted your own nature it is easier to accept and coexist with everyone else's nature. And some may see this as a form of manipulation and others may see this is operating in the most efficient manner. For example, if your child is of the opposite sex and they at some point choose to live with you. Do you have what it takes to teach a young girl how to be a woman with or without a support system?

Next you need to know the parent that you co-parenting with. Once you get to know their nature you will begin to understand how they operate. This understanding of each other's nature in a positive way could build an ideal situation for child development. In a negative way it can be a recipe for disaster. So you have to know their parenting ideologies and how to effectively work with them. It may be easy to get on the same page or you may have to appeal to their own interests for your child's best interest. Some people are ready and able to step up to the plate. Others need a bit of persuasion. You don't have to play games and manipulate moments to find out a person's nature. They will actively show you in their actions what they are about and who they are. Once you find this out your next move is to figure out how these things can be used for your child's benefit in the long run. And always be clear about your and the other parent's responsibilities and expectations. Accountability will be a two-way street.

Then you have to figure out the support systems. Because of the number of people that may be involved this may take more time. When you're talking about family and friends you have to figure out who are the people who will be most consistent with interaction with your child. Everybody has some type of screening process to build trust with someone. Sort of a probationary period. You know some people are good at taking care of babies and other people a good at grooming children become to adults. Once you get the hang of that you figure out who's the best fit for the particular circumstance. And like everything else it's a bit of trial and error during this process because people can change over time. Always remember that they are your support system which means they do not have the final say as a parent, you do. Conversely, be able to take the advice of someone who has more wisdom than you do in a particular area of parenting.

After that you have to learn the nature of society. Society views and treats parents differently with numerous stances. There will be certain gender biases, age biases, class biases, race biases, and opinions. You may find yourself in a place where people are overly concerned about your parenting when you're doing a fine job. Or you may find yourself in a place where people are completely apathetic to you doing a poor job of parenting. Over time you will have to know and understand your surroundings. Usually you have to use your intellect to read between the lines because human interaction when it comes to parenting has been declining for years. People might not want to get involved to help the situation out of fear and past bad experiences. So the onus is on you to gauge the society you are in at the moment you are in it. Trust in your common sense, intelligence, and instincts.

And last but not least know your child. Know how they

communicate and why they communicate the way they do. Know their nature and things that they are advanced on as well is the things they are impulsive about. Pay attention to them so you can be able to read their emotions and help them work through those emotions. Be open enough with them so they can understand your nature as a person not just as a parent. Be open to being the first teacher of self-awareness. It is definitely a process that is rooted in constant evolution. You're going to need to know what makes your child tick. The difference between them telling the truth and telling a lie. The things that they are confident about as well as the things that they are insecure about. You just have to remember that though you share the same DNA you will not be completely the same. So as well as loving your child you have to study them. Once you begin to get a grasp of who they are you will begin to understand how to motivate them, build up their confidence, teach perseverance, and all the necessary things that good parenting entails to create an exceptional adult.

Let It All Play Out

Life happens, so you should not be overly emotional about the things that happen in it. In due time all things work themselves out because that is the nature of life. No feast or famine can last forever. So what is needed is patience and understanding. As an adult you have the ability to look back and see how much you have grown since you were a child. Give your child the same opportunity to go through the peaks and valleys in the different phases that coincide with growth. This is also partially a trust exercise in self and parenting ability. You need to be able to step back and let it all play out.

When a child is young they need your presence for constant guidance. But as they get older they get more and more independent. With each new experience there is a new set of obstacles that would test your child's life skills. You begin to gauge how much of an input you need to put forth in certain situations by the level of trust you have in your child's decision-making. My grandmother once told me a story about my father. She told me when he was younger they had a talk because she was a bit overprotective. In this talk he asked her a question. "How do you kill a butterfly?" She was kind of puzzled by the question. He began to tell her that if you catch a butterfly and hold it in your hands for too long you'll kill it. You see you may like butterflies but their natural habitat is not in your hands or a jar. So you have to love something enough to let it go and that it be what it is.

So of course we as parents have to begin to tow the line between protection and freedom. There are certain situations where our advice or guidance will be completely overlooked. There comes a point when that's okay because experience is sometimes the best teacher even when it's unnecessary. You see when you're a parent, you're a parent for life. The journey that you are on and the path that you set will be one that your child will follow. Your experiences in life outside of parenting are an active blueprint to what will happen and how to respond to it in life. The beauty of your age is wisdom. The understanding of the system of life. It is through your past experience that you are able to look at the bigger picture and give a complete overview. That is why you have the ability to let it all play out because you are a living map of the peaks and valleys.

Certain family and friends are not your family and friends. Certain ideologies do not work out in the real world. There are certain places that you should not go. In life you will reap what you sow. But with that being said within those experiences that you have encountered you know the level of danger that each situation can escalate to. So by you as a parent assessing the risk you can also determine to the degree of which you involve yourself with each situation as it is unfolding. Of course there will be times that you have to save your child from themselves. They may not understand that at the moment but they will thank you later. But they'll also be other times you have to let them succeed or fail on their own merit. Because they need the opportunity to trust themselves and their own decision-making. If that is taken away from them, it will damage their life skills because they will always have to be told what to do out of the fear of not trusting their own instincts or experience.

Just think about it logically, you have kids that grow up to be productive adults and you have kids that are stuck and arrested development. The kids that grow up to be productive adults have a certain level of self-confidence because of their accomplishments. Those accomplishments came from being able to make choices and deal with the results of those choices. They learned to listen to the guidance but also learned the lesson of using principles to guide themselves on the trail that they will blaze for their own lives. Which by the way, may make your child gravitate to you more as they get older and choose to live with you because of the sincere guidance and practice of decision making. The kids that are stuck in arrested development have a harder time coping with life because they are always waiting for someone to step in and help. When they make mistakes you help them fix it which is a bad idea. When they are successful in something you are there helping every step of the way which sabotages their self-confidence. You see there comes a point where you have to let that butterfly spread its wings and fly. If you do you won't need to hold it in both of your hands or catch it with a net because it will fly to you and land on you on its own because you're comfortable place to call home.

Live Beneath Your Means.

Budgeting is an important facet of being able to survive or thrive in any financial situation. So with that being said, you may have to follow certain rules of budgeting. Using worst-case scenario or planning for growth in the future it might be wise to live below your means instead of within them. If you are reading this. I'm sure you are one of those parents or know one of those parents who winds up paying for things two or three times. So this lesson is particularly for the parents who wind up spending extra all the time while they're providing and paying child support. When it comes to little girls and little boys you are, or know one of those noncustodial parents who knows that when they see their child they're going to look a mess. It could be hygiene, clothes, over or underweight, or any other type of subpar situation.

Here are some things that can ease the financial strain on the way. Set up a small bank account for your child on the side. Every couple of weeks put a set amount in it. Or if there's something major that they want to do start putting a set amount in advance to pay for it before that day comes. This way you are preparing for the excuses you may or may not get about splitting the cost of something. So when it comes to things like clothing, I found the easiest thing to do is to buy the size up when the clothing is out of season. So in the summer buy winter clothes because they're cheaper at the time and vice versa when it comes to the winter. As a bonus when you are shopping pick up underwear and socks in the same fashion. The reason is you can get cheap apparel that is quality but also get a bargain and maybe even a clearance sale. I'm sure you're no stranger to your children coming over to your home with old clothes. Usually, the routine is they come with nothing and they want to leave with everything. If you participate in this, you will be buying new clothing forever. So the practical thing to do is to stockpile clothing and every now and then they can take something back. But if they leave with it don't expect it to come back and don't expect it to come back in good shape. So make sure it's something that's clean but has a little bit of mileage on it. Now the same process applies when it comes to shoes.

Another reason for the side fund is in the advent that your child wants to participate in extracurricular activities. There's been plenty of times when two parents strike up a deal to go half or switch payments monthly and someone doesn't hold up their end of the bargain. So just in case that happens you have a sit down with your child and tell them how you pay for that extracurricular activity. That way they know and they will not bug you about it because they know you did your part. Now if the bad deals persist then you may have to have another conversation with your child. If it is something that they really want to participate in and you are able to facilitate that, then you two can strike up a deal (meaning parent and child). Within this context you might want to let them know that the next activity that they want to participate in will be the other parent's responsibility. Now of course this could come with some kind of backlash because some parents don't want to be responsible for their child's endeavors. But the living beneath your means is a way to plan ahead and cover the cost of certain activities that you as a parent may feel that your child has earned. Sometimes it doesn't matter who pays what rather that the good behavior deserves positive reinforcement.

When it comes to visitation or planned events this fund also may come in handy. Some people may purposely be a no-show at things that are already planned for them to attend. If things like this happen use your trusty smart phone to record the event, take pictures, and gently break it to your child that it did happen. Because sometimes within the back-and-forth someone is bound to lie so use your friend technology to debunk the myth. The same goes for flight reservations because under normal circumstances you can get reimbursed and use the funds for plane ticket on another flight if you pay extra for the flight insurance. But there are circumstances where people do not tell you that they're not putting your child on a plane and you just lost time and money. Use technology for the same thing. Whether you take that to court or not that's a decision you have to make on your own. Even if this is a habit the likelihood of them changing the custody agreement is minimal. The custodial parent will probably just get a slap on the wrist. So to save yourself some of the frustration, pay into that little side fund in advance for these type of events.

For those who don't have to worry about these type of problems that little side fund goes great with family experiences. You already have a miscellaneous fund to use on whatever activity you see fit. You want to take them to the game, concert, museums, movies, etc., just using that extra cushion alone frees some things up. One of the coolest things you may be able to do is to redecorate your child's room with them. Maybe they want to paint the walls, get a new bedroom set, and let their personality shine in their room. If you've been putting money in that little fund for the consistent amount of time you don't have to spend money, it's already there. Now I will have to warn you that living beneath your means may still cause a certain uproar with certain types. Because then your child may say all the fun things they did and someone might start calculating how much was spent and think they should apply for an increase. At that point you are still comfortable because you live below your means but you still live well and it exposes where some people's true intentions are for the way that they parent. Plus, they will just be wasting their time. Moving on to another important thing. Your monthly cost increase. Your bills may go up a little bit, like your kid my like ordering On Demand movies. So it also prepares you to take that little hit. Nothing major but it's well worth it and for some new parents it's something that they need to know. Just like this prepares you for Christmas and any other holiday season you already have your shopping money and you might not have to work overtime to get it. And as is written previously if you have a great working relationship with the other parent this is also a great way to put money aside for college or a car. The earlier you start the less you may have to put in but it adds up in the end.

Living below your means doesn't mean living a poor or impoverished lifestyle. It is just the way to start small and grow big while you're raising your child. Due to the fact that it seems to be more difficult nowadays to scale back from a lifestyle that you're comfortable with then to grow into one that's bigger. So part of the premise is to continuously grow while planning to take a few hits along the way. Just like every business knows it will to take a loss at some point and they predict it and calculate about how much will be lost. You have to be your own business and go through the books to see what works that will consistently keep you in the black. Plus, it is very difficult for a child accustomed to a certain lifestyle to maintain it because you haven't taught them the skills to provide it for themselves. They will only become angry and entitled which as an adult is not productive. If they see constant growth then they can put together that hard work and planning always pay off in the end. Because if you look around society we start small, grow big, and then streamline to our specifications. So it may be best to get to the streamlining because it makes effective and efficient use of finances and those finances create freedom that parents and children can bond within.

Also find ways of making money outside of your primary income. Learn how to invest, trade stocks, or turn a passion into a business. Find a way to create different streams of income so you can give yourself some financial freedom. Allow yourself to start small and grow for not only you but for your child. Working overtime is good but you don't want to work yourself into an early grave trying to provide the things that your child needs at the present time. You may want to use this as a way to fund college, trips, and other events. Be aware that a financial increase in these things may be grounds for an increase in child support. So what! It doesn't last forever. Also this is a tactic that can generate passive income just in case you are given custody in the teenage years under the idea of building a better relationship. When in fact it can also be a way to put you in position to be responsible for college expenses. Which by the way, you may be able to use your W-2 to make your child an in state student. The good thing is by this time you will have taught your child the importance of hard and smart work. It will be a good age to start putting the lessons in practice and gaining experience.

Make Lots of Lemonade

Some of us may feel like we've gotten a raw deal. When you feel that way remember that old saying "When life gives you lemons, make lemonade." Whether it's realistic or perceived you can always make the best out of a bad situation. We live in a culture where we glorify winners but also root for the underdogs. So with that being said it is possible to turn your weaknesses into your strengths in order to maximize your potential. This same principle can easily be applied when parenting. What I'm going to do is give you a few examples of how you can make the best of a bad situation.

In the area of communication with the child. Sometimes it can be a difficult process. This is one of the reasons why I believe in consistently reaching out. Because there comes a point when your child knows that it's normal for you to check on their well-being on an everyday basis. For some of us this is a welcomed with open arms for others it is not. So for those who are getting stonewalled it is a perfect opportunity to create projects. For instance, if you see or talk to your child on a Monday and you've noticed that you may not be able to see or talk to them for days or weeks at a time. What you do is give them something to think about and do. It could be something as simple as reading a book and giving a book report. Maybe teach them a card trick and reconnecting to see if they've gotten it right. Or even have them set a workout goal and see if they were able to reach it or surpass it. This is a way to build a bond and help in their progression as a person.

When it comes to cultivating responsibility the opportunity is also present. One normal thing that most parents have an issue with is getting a child to respect other people's property and to respect their own. So one of the easiest ways to do that is to make them work and earn the things that they want. In doing so you can mutually come up with a plan of action and execute it together. Even in coming up with a plan you both can come to an agreement and compromise on the best approach and layout both party's responsibilities. For example, maybe your child wants a cell phone. You may not feel that their responsible enough to take care of it and don't want to create another bill. But at the same time you may feel that you do need to figure out another avenue outside of the parent to be able to communicate. So this is where the idea of purchasing some type of tablet comes into play. Because normally your child may want a phone just to have one to play games on. So on a tablet you can play games, but you can also use the Internet to Skype. Understanding that, they may only take care of what they put in for so you strike a deal to pay half if they come up with the other half. Of course I would include some type of protector to make sure they don't drop it or break it in the beginning. If they agree to the deal they are probably more prone to take care of it and not be as reckless. If not, it would definitely be a valuable lesson learned because they will also lose out on the work they put into getting it.

One of the daily constants in your child's life will be education. There certain subjects that they are good in and certain subjects they may not be as good in. This creates an opportunity to spark the interest on why these things are important and be able to show them another side of you. Sometimes because the parent and child are so similar in certain ways you may be able to teach something in the way you learned it so that they can get it. Whether it's in the STEM field or history your previous knowledge and wisdom in those subjects can be used to create a level of trust and understanding to the guidance that you can provide. So even if you not able to have as active of a role as you would like, there will always come a point when your child has to reach out for your help and in that moment of availability you are planting another seed of trust.

Using the lemonade analogy cooking is one of the simplest ways to figuratively make lemonade. If you practice on cooking and you get good at it, I can guarantee your child will love something that you make. And the great thing about that is that if they like it they'll want it. So at some point they will ask you to teach them how to make it. Whether it's face-to-face or over the telephone the experience will be unforgettable. Because not only are you teaching them something that they will love, you also teaching them something that they will re-create with their children. That is the beauty of making lemonade.

Moving Parts

This is a figurative and literal topic. Along the journey you will find yourself in somewhat of a jigsaw puzzle. Every piece to fit the puzzle may not be the same so you have to figure out which pieces are correct. This is why I didn't write this in chapters and I wrote it more so in topics. There will always be something the plan for, consequences of past teachings, and future mindsets to contend with. Being the navigator of the situation is a completely thankless job because you may be the only person who can see the horizon from your vantage point. Others may take years to catch up. So let's just get into the parts.

You may have to contend with constant moving from city to city or school to school which has you constantly playing a game of catch-up. Which actually may be good grounds to stand on get primary custody by the way if that is a problem. This issue may lead to future issues such as a child's lack of expression towards another human being due to the fact that they may get accustomed to people not lasting in their lives. Similar to the model of military kids who move from state to state. Because there are some who have to deal with the constant disappearing act and that act can create a constant division between one parent and one child. Some may even grow up to be nomadic because constant uprooting is normalcy. Which may lead to a child having adult relationship problems. A healthy relationship needs structure and stability just like parenting.

As for stability, if you have a constant tug-of-war your child will grow up to be in a constant tug-of-war. And as an adult it will look as such, mother versus father versus child. The problem with having three different mentalities to solve one problem is having three different mentalities assume that their right because of their own bias. In this situation it becomes extremely difficult to actually figure out what works. Because success or failure may be also tied into emotional connections or disconnections between the parent-child dynamic. This is why telling a child to undermine the other parent becomes an issue for children as an adult. You may put them in worst-case scenario of taking bad advice because they love someone more which puts them in an unsuccessful position that they will harbor resentment for one parent and direct misplaced hate toward another. At the same time multiply their insecurities or inability to have self-reliance.

Now let's get into all the people and parts involved. You have parents, grandparents, extended family, educational figures, athletic figures, religious figures, legal figures, neighbors, society, and friends. All of them have different types of relationships with the parents and the children that will grow or die over time and circumstances. You may not know who has the biggest impact or the most profound life lessons outside of yourselves as parents. Life is unpredictable like that. People may come in with the best of intentions or the worst of intentions to increase the positivity or enhance the negativity. This is part of the reason why parenting is a situational endeavor. With so many things that can happen from the prelude of an event to the aftermath you have to be prepared for all aspects of life. The constant change of life is also a cornerstone to the evolution of the parent-child relationship. You may have the wisdom given to you by your experiences but that may not be the same type of wisdom that can be translated properly. This is where some of the moving parts of people and situations become more relevant.

In order to guide your child in the right direction you may have to work with, work through, work around, and not work at all with the moving parts. At the end of the day the only thing that matters is the results. The positive results of what's in your child's best interest. How you get to those results and who you work with to get to those results are what you would have to figure out. This is an honest and ego free zone. It's okay to call in a ringer. It's okay to let life knock the child down. It's okay to put up traffic lights, guardrails, signs, and roadblocks to assure them a safe journey through life with or without them knowing that you were ahead of them doing construction. If you can't get the reference an old saying is "It's okay to plan for their safety ahead of time with or without them knowing."

Think in order for them to be successful they have to see successful. In order to see success, you have to expose them to a three-dimensional thought process. The thing about being young is you think in linear terms. So if you're good you get Christmas gifts and if you're bad you don't. But it's going to come a time when you're going to have to expose them to the things that they don't see that coincide with the things that they do see. It is a simple as the learning of history. You study the past to see how it affects the present so it gives you the ability to predict the future. You as a parent are the culmination of the history that surrounds you. Your child is that exact same thing. The dot in the middle of a circle that has different experiences gravitating to them from all 360°. So as you will use the tools surrounding you to create the best possible experience for yourself you will also have to use that experience to teach your child how to maneuver all of the moving parts of life for their best interest.

So treat it like a game of chess. Your child is the king, parents are the queen, family are the bishops, friends are the knights, mentors are the rooks, and teachers are the pawns. Your opponent is life and you make your moves according to put life in checkmate.

Parenting Forward

Paying it forward as a parent so your children don't have to repeat the cycle is the premise. Every experience that you may go through is not only a learning experience but a cycle breaking experience. Take a look at the way society is structured and functioning. It seems to be a generational rerun with different characters but the same story. So part of your experience is to notice what has to be passed down to not repeat the same storyline or what will write a different ending. We can tell it's the same because we are viewing numerous different individuals repeating the same mistakes without taking heed to the guidance of those who previously traveled the exact same road. Which falls in line with the definition of *insanity*- repeating the same things over and over again and expecting a different result.

Let's look at dating for example. You have a growing generation of men that want to be married and a growing generation of women want to be married, but they may not be marriage material. We evolved into a consummate hookup culture where commitment seems to be the goal but at the same time few have the ability to cohesively work together with the opposite sex. Within this framework you see divorce at around 50%, the rise of children out of wedlock growing, and a culture that promotes a brewing hatred for the opposite sex. Within this backdrop the question is, who is your child going to date? And what is the probability that they will get married and have children within a stable marriage? So in this paradigm it may be best for us as parents do the best we can to show our children how to have a functional relationship with the opposite sex. Because if we don't all that we can be is failed parents turned nervous grandparents participating out of guilt. In life there are no guarantees, but that doesn't mean you get to omit the logic of paving a smooth road for your future generations to ride on. You see part of the problem is the fact that we forget to parent our children for interacting with the opposite sex in a functional manner. So take your children out on dates to teach them how to date and how they behave on dates. That way they know the proper way to treat people and how to be treated. Because if your son or daughter brings home somebody that you are not comfortable with. It could be out of rebellion, or it could be that they were taught that dysfunction was attractive. No matter the case the buck has to stop somewhere. And one of the ways to stop that buck is to show them how to treat the opposite sex with some respect, dignity, and honesty. Whether your child goes down the path of marriage or single life they will not see the opposite sex as the enemy and re-create a dysfunctional environment that their kids will grow up into and think is normal.

Let's look at work ethic for an example. In this microwavable fast food culture, we are seeing longevity becoming a thing of the past. People are not working as hard or as smart as they once did in the past. Instead of being focused on being excellent and well balanced all across the board. We are dealing with a culture of specialists who are not equipped to deal with the totality of whatever expertise that they claim to be well-versed in. It's kind of like watching a basketball game and you see players who can shoot but can't dribble or pass. They can play defense but they can't play offense. Their great when they go to the right but below average when they go to the left. Which as far as parenting goes it makes it the best of times and the worst of times. Because it doesn't take as much as it used to in effort to be able to produce an excellent child. Yet at the same time the mentality and ability to maintain a high level of production is not required in this society. Slowly but surely when you concede to mediocrity in one way it will surely spill into another. This is why you pay it forward with parenting and with work ethic. If you don't, you surely will be parenting your grandchildren because mediocre parenting creates children with mediocre parenting skills. In this process you always have to teach the value and payoff of hard work and dedication. Nothing worth having will come by taking the easiest road possible. And nothing worth keeping will be able to maintain itself on that road. Think about it in your own life. How many times have you seen people who never left the nest and the family was scared to push them out to become adults? At the least you internally told yourself I'm glad that's not me. And a sure-fire way to make sure this is not you is to have a consistent work ethic that produces a lifestyle that your children could see themselves living. You see they may not choose the same career path issue, but they will associate being able to turn a passion into an income or business or finding a career that facilitates a favorable lifestyle while pursuing a passion. Either way, with their own eyes they will see that you get out of life what you put into it.

As far as dealing with parenting or co-parenting they would have a blueprint. They can look back on their own childhood and say to themselves they know what father did right and what mother did right. So if they know it worked for them that they can apply to their own children with great confidence that it will work too. In dealing with marriage, divorce, or two different households they will have a working model of what to do and what not to do. You see one of the biggest elephants in the room that is often overlooked is that children don't choose their parents but as adults they choose the relationship they will have with their parents. The reason for that, is when your child becomes an adult and becomes a parent they can immediately decipher what really happened in situations in their childhood. And it is at that point when they figure out who was responsible and the intentions behind their actions. Now on which side of the fence you land will be between you and your child when they have children. So in this scenario parenting forward is putting their best interests at heart and taking the high road for their future even when it hurts your present. In that you can't expect the kid to understand what you did and why you did it until they grow up. When it comes to children, emotions run high and people make hasty decisions that have a domino effect because most parents have selective memories about creating. So when emotions run high or you are feeling like you getting the short end of the stick you may want to take a minute to calm down and not process how it can affect your present but rather your children and grandchildren's future. That way you can effectively respond to situations with foresight and not reactively respond to situations that you may regret in hindsight.

As far as bonding goes, make the most out of every experience. Treat parenting the same way people tell you to treat life. Do it as if this will be your last day ever. Have fun and make memories. Be in a loving competition with all of the great things that you remember from your childhood and top those moments. If you do that your child will in turn want to re-create those same moments with their child. In this process the beauty is actually the journey because you really don't know what experience is going to be the one that they carry with them for life. Looking back, I remember my first wrestling match, football game, favorite television shows with a parent, my favorite dish, and a host of other things that can put a smile on my face on a rainy day. I've seen those reminiscing moments that re-create joy over and over again. It is those moments that when you become a parent you want your child to experience over and over again. It adds a great sense of pride knowing that you once received the moment and now you are able to give it. That great moment plans to repeat itself for your children to create great moments which is a gift that keeps on giving. You see if you can make parenting forward a family tradition we can one by one change the dynamics of our society.

The most important parenting forward idea is the concept of passing down something. For fathers' specifically because we are men, the ideal of legacy is always on our conscious. To fulfill their legacy, you have to build something, create something, own something, or harness something that you can pass down to the next generation. You know the simplest of these is the old when you turn 16 you get a car. Kids see it as a car, but really it's the idea of passing down the responsibility from one generation to the next. To be able to have a legacy, you have to have the next generation in mind to give it to. As parents that is one of the fundamental proving grounds of the work that you put in as a parent. You see we all know this is a cold cruel world. And if it's true that we know this, we have to do whatever it is in our power to do to provide our children a leg up in a world that will show them no mercy. There is an extreme amount of respect that men will give a King who was able to build his own castle. But I can guarantee you that that same King will not tell his heirs to go out and build another kingdom because they are set to inherit one.

Plant the Principles

Using a gardening reference about planting seeds. You have to clear the path to plant the seeds and to protect the seeds so they can grow. Once you do that you can let nature take its course. This is pretty much the same model for planting the principles that will be paramount to development. We all have had situation with telling our child the same thing over and over again. Yes, it is an exhausting and repetitive process but it is necessary. Normally at some point life will intervene and the lesson will bloom into a reality for your child to understand. Part of the problem sometimes is the lack of consistency. So in order to circumvent some of life's inevitable problems it may be a good idea to plant the principles that will ensure success. There are plenty of mottos in the world. "Go hard or go home." "If God can't trust you with the small things he will never trust you with the big." "Perfect practice makes perfect." "Honesty is the best policy." "Reach for the stars, if you miss you'll land on the moon." "Trust your instincts." just to name a few.

"Go hard to go home." We all know this to be a reference of giving 100% when involving yourself in an activity. If you're not in it all the way, there is no reason for you to be in it. This is a very important principle because it applies to work ethic and performance. The motto itself eludes to either making a difference or going home until you're willing to make a difference. Which can be a great framework to teach a child how to do their homework, compete, and various other aspects of life. Now once this seed is planted life will do the rest. Because ultimately this is based in competition. And there will be something in life that your child wants to be the best at. With that being said you can only be the best by giving your all. So if ever there is a moment of disappointment the energy can be channeled into "Going harder."

"If God can't trust you with the small things he will never trust you with the big." The simplest form of this would be doing your chores. Basically chores are nothing more than preparation for child a to become an adult and take care of themselves. They learn how to wash the dishes because they going to have to wash their own dishes. They learn how to clean their rooms because they're going to have to clean their own room. The same goes for washing clothes, budgeting, grooming, cooking, working, and the list goes on and on. The one constant is that they will have to do it for themselves. So this motto is a quote for self-sufficiency. It's pretty much the same model as schooling. You learn and then you graduate to the next level. So along the way there will be a few bumps in the road. And this happens because people try to take shortcuts. We all learn that shortcuts usually don't work out with long-term situations. Financially they may learn that it is better to pay for something one time that may be expensive, than to pay for something numerous times at a cheaper rate. Which brings up property. You don't continue to buy a child toys that they break on purpose. So when they ask for a bigger toy or better toy the answer should be "No". The normal response is

"Why?" and then the normal reply is "Because you didn't take care of the last one." Now from this point I can do the whole back-and-forth, but we all know how the rest goes. Yet the lesson is still once you learn how to take care of your things, you'll graduate to be able to get better things.

"Perfect practice makes perfect." Revisiting this analogy because it's very simple. You don't master anything by the mediocre practice of it. If you're actually passionate about something, you will be passionate about it when you practice it. Before every show there is a rehearsal. If the rehearsal is good the show is probably going to be good. Now if the rehearsal is bad the show is going to probably be bad. The same goes for learning. If the subject doesn't interest someone they are lackadaisical in the way they approach it. Which normally never leads to good results. So if somebody complains that they didn't get a good grade or they could've done better, it is usually because their practice lacked effort. Effort is one of the key things in life that separates bad from good and good from great. When your child is witnessing greatness they may have the tendency to ask how did someone get that good. Usually the blanket response is that they practiced on it a lot. So in a roundabout way, you are letting them know they're only as good as the work if they're willing to put in. Which is why you have to emphasize that the work you put in has to be at the same level as the results you want to get from it.

"Honesty is the best policy." Because we live in a culture that is okay with lying and manipulating to get ahead the value of honesty is often overlooked. But ultimately honesty brings peace while dishonesty breeds turmoil. There is a certain level of respect that we all have for people who are honest even if they are brutally honest. That is due to the fact that we don't have to waste time deciphering through all of the BS that goes with lying. Plus, there really isn't a reason to communicate with someone who is dishonest. Honest people are easy to talk to and easier to be friends with. When you plant the seeds of honesty you can always move on to the next subject. You won't find yourself having to double back and fix something that was based in a lie. Also dishonesty breeds contempt because in these days, dishonest people run out of options fast and wind up right in front of the people that they have lied to. So teach and reward truth. The saying "The truth set shall set you free." has stood the test of time. That is for very a significant reason. And the antithesis of that is lies leave a person in bondage. Because they are still trapped in the hell that they've created for themselves with their own lies. So as a parent is important to teach your child to be free.

"Reach for the stars, if you miss you land on the moon." We all have dreams, so why not teach our children to dream big. When I was a kid we used to play like we were superheroes. The thing about it was only one person could be Superman. But I remember no one had a problem being Batman, Hulk, Aquaman, Spiderman, or any other hero we picked. That was because at the end of the day we were all still super. So if you dream for greatness and you fall short that doesn't mean that you are not great. It only means you didn't achieve your dream level yet. So when it's all said and done make sure your child knows that if they aren't Superman they are still super.

"Trust your instincts." We teach children about their five senses. You know touch, taste, sight, smell, and sound. Somewhere along the way we forget to tell them about their instincts. That gut feeling that you get that something is going to work out or is not going to work. It is in that trust of self that you grow confident in your own abilities. We are all different and we are all special, so that means we all have gifts specific to who we are. What we must do is cultivate our trust in self. When you plant the seed for your child to trust themselves they will become more responsible and more aware of self and surroundings. Some of the greatest people in the history of mankind had in unwavering belief in their own abilities. You have to remember you are the only you that there will ever be. So the things that are especially you, you should not be ashamed of. Rather embrace your differences because they make you unique and free you to be the you that you were born to be. So if it feels right listen to that inner voice and if it feels wrong listen to that inner voice. But ultimately begin to trust and believe in the inner voice. And you may have to teach this lesson by demonstrating your uniqueness to your child.

Stay The Course

For many of us the hardest things to do is staying the course. You will have many ups and downs and frustrating experiences that you won't see immediate payoff for. Because of this it has been a normal thing to disassociate yourself from the co-parenting situation until your child *is* old enough to reach out to you and you'll begin to build a relationship from there. The problem with that is this. That only works some of the times because some children don't want an explanation after certain age. They are completely done and checked out of allowing you to be a parent because of your disappearance. So the degree of that working is in between an educated guess and a crapshoot. In practical application staying the course is usually the best route. Due to the fact that the consistency of your actions will always be taken into consideration even if they are met with obstacles.

Look at your parenting as a mirror of the story *The Tortoise and The Hare.* In this parenting situation you are *The Tortoise.* Even though in the beginning there was logically no reason you should be able to win the race, but if you stay the course you will cross the finish line first. The reasoning behind that is this. If you put your child's best interests first, it puts you in a position to constantly go one step at a time. See sometimes being the custodial parent can be frustrating because you may need a break. But it can also create an environment of procrastination because of the daily routine. So what you have to do is accept the fact that you'll be taking small steps and not making great strides in the beginning.

Now just like *The Hare* logically the victory was a sure thing. It had every advantage to win a race against *The Tortoise*. But fortunately for the Tortoise it was never really about winning the race to the Hare. So the advantages are very simple. Family Court, governmental support systems, societal biases, time, and control of the narrative. The only problem with that is this, those same advantages are still not used to win the race. The race being putting your child on a fast track to success in life. So along the way *The Hare* is going to get off the path of the race, go to a party or two, and fall asleep. And it is in that procrastination that those small steps start to turn into huge strides. Plus, the beauty of it is the strides happen inside of the race where it really matters. So if you're looking to win the race or you're looking for glory. Either way if you take it step by step you will be the winner.

Just for the purpose of fairness I have to say that the goal is really to run the race together and be on the same page. Some children have two Hares, some have two Tortoises, and some have one of each. In an ideal world it would be better if they were to run a relay instead of a race. In a relay you pass the baton to your teammate who is better equipped for that part of the race but ultimately the team finishes the race together. Meaning if you're able to delegate responsibility to who can run the race better at that particular time. Pass the baton and get the win. Because in an ideal sense parenting is a relay team not an individual race. That being said, even the best relay teams have to find the best order to run in for the best results for the team to win. So ultimately, find out who you are in that story and what your role is in the race. And unlike the fairytale if you don't like a character you can always switch roles.

Teach Them How To Fish

"Give a man a fish and he will eat for a day, teach a man to fish and he will eat for lifetime." I think I got it right verbatim but you get the point. This is a very important subject that society is currently paying for. As children are becoming overly aggressive, disrespectful, hypersexual, indignant, and a list of other traits that just equate to them being dysfunctional. All of this stems from one thing. Most of these children have no skills. It's not just that they have too much time on their hands, it is that they were never taught anything productive to do with that time. As parents that's where we step in. All of us want our children to grow up and be something better than us, but the fallacy is in not teaching them what we learned how to be. Children will always grow and evolve to choose their own path. But what you have to do is give them options of paths to take. Just because we see somebody excellent and successful in one particular genre doesn't mean that they are not excellent at things that are completely different. All it means is that this particular field of expertise paid more than the other.

One major thing that we have to get over as parents is caring about our children's feelings when it comes to teaching them a skill. You may not want your daughter fixing cars, but if her car broke down you have to hope that somebody is willing to help her and not take advantage of the situation. So if you have the ability to teach her, she could probably get herself out of a jam and that pride as a parent along with the boost of self-confidence for your daughter will be well worth the aggravation of teaching the skill of mechanics. Now of course we're not preparing Navy SEALs for war. But similar to their training, they are given all the tools to survive under any circumstance before they go off to battle. So in my opinion it is best to give your child every tool you can feasibly give them to prepare for life. Though I do understand that gender roles will apply in certain circumstances. The difference with that is in the mindset and application of how to do things differently for their success in whatever the skill is that you can teach.

When it comes to things that outside of your wheelhouse of expertise that's when you get creative. There are plenty of things people can teach to children outside of the framework of a private or public education. Normally the question is, how long will this particular interest hold your child's attention and how much would it cost? In this paradigm will have to do a little saving and planning. At some point children talk to you and tell you what interests them and what they want to do. It is at that point that you make the decision to test their seriousness and enforce that they will see it completely through. One of the biggest mistakes that I see most parents make is they let their children give up on things too easily because it's hard. The easiest way to figure out if they've lost interest or they're scared is to pay attention to the confidence when they achieve something in this particular interest. If they are successful at something and you see that spark in their eyes and a smile on her face, you know that they think they can do it despite their doubts. But if they succeed and are still nonchalant it may be pretty much over with that particular interest. Even in that circumstance make sure you see it completely through until its end. You don't want to create a child that can walk away from anything at any time.

Be willing to go BIG! For example, maybe save up for flights lessons. Teenagers can be pilots. You'll challenge their intellect and have them complete things completely outside the box of what their peers are doing. While simultaneously giving them a skill that can be used to turn into a career if they ever ran out of options. You see once you give someone a skill it is something that they can carry with them for the rest of their lives. Think about it, how many adults that you know forgot how to ride a bike? Going big is also confidence builder. You may not have a pilot's license but your child may be enthusiastic to tell you all about the friendly skies. With those conversations about new experiences and mental growth are always good for child and for the parent who's proud of a successful experience.

The ultimate reason in teaching the skill is to rest easy at night. Some parents worry about what is going to happen to their children when they get into the real world. But hypothetically speaking if your child knows how to invest, budget, save, shop, cook, clean, defend themselves, fly a plane, fix a car, do home repairs, run a business, and be aware of their surroundings. You pretty much don't have too many things to worry about. Along the way they will pick up a skill from someone else. That will only add to whatever success that they are participating in. And it is at that point that you can also comfortably take a look into the future about the things that your grandchildren will be able to learn. So ultimately you are working to a win-win situation. And one perk of winning is that your child will always come back with reverence and be thankful for the foundation of skills that they are able to pull from that will help them build a better life. Which makes parenting all the more worthwhile.

Technology can be your friend.

In the past, there were plenty of adults who had problems communicating with a child about past situations. Due to the advances in technology that is no longer the case. There are plenty of steps you can take to communicate efficiently and effectively with your child at any given time because of technology. First, you can set up an email address. With this email address you can send yourself emails with the explicit purpose of giving your child all the information that was missed out with miscommunication over the years. Such as times, dates, scenarios, trips, visitation, and the list can go on and on. By using this email address when your child is of age give them the password and let them look at everything that was done that you may have not been able to verbalize so they can understand or so they can see the proof with their own eyes without having to have an argument.

With the introduction of smart phones, computers, and all of the applications that can be used you have a plethora of options to be able to communicate effectively with your child. As in the past, the basis was pretty much you can call, come by, or they can come to you. Now you can call, visit, Skype, tango, Facebook, FaceTime, Snapchat, Hangout, email, text, tweet, and whatever technology will be available to do in the future. The best part about all this technology is this. It is all synchronized to the point where dates and times are involved in every interaction. You can screenshot any conversation via text. So no longer do you have to live in a world filled with hearsay. Which in due time creates a healthy situation and environment for communication and trust with a child, because instead of believing what somebody says or what somebody didn't say the proof is always available. Knowing this paradigm, you have plenty of scenarios and situations where things can work in your favor or against you. You may have to ask yourself some serious tough questions.

- How much of this information will I remember?
- Under which situations is the use of technology appropriate?
- Does everything have to be recorded?
- Which information is for the best interest of the child?
- How far am I willing to go with this?
- How can I use this technology for the better?
- Does my child know the reason behind why I have to use forms of technology?

In the advent you may be going through a custody battle. Your conversations may be recorded. If you are one of those fathers who are trying to figure out why your child is disrespectful, evasive, or omitting information, you may be getting baited into a trap. You see the recording conversations without the other person's knowledge in some states is legal and other states it's illegal. But that's in a conversation between two consenting adults. When having a conversation with your child there is a loophole that you can talk to your child and somebody can record the conversation on the phone even though you thought it was private. So if you ever feel like you have to discipline your child verbally over the telephone for bad behavior or bad manners it also may be because you being goaded into disciplining your child and being looked upon as a verbally abusive parent. On the opposite side of the spectrum, you may have to use that same type of technology to protect yourself because some people have conversations and they may edit conversations to look a certain way in front of people. That is if you're in the scenario of a custody battle.

One of the first things you need to do using technology is to create a schedule. Figure out a feasible time to communicate with the child on a regular basis. In that time frame it will be known that this is the time that we communicate within whatever form of communication you've agreed upon. That way at a certain time they will know that you're reaching out and if they missed that time for whatever reason they can call back. In this scenario you have to initiate all of the communication process simply because you are the parent and that is part of your job. Now in the advent that you are not able to communicate with your child in the circumstances that's where technology comes to cover you. See if you call using telephone plans, cell phones give you at least 12 months of phone records to refer back to on your plan. So if you call and you constantly get a no answer. You download 12 months of calls from the call logs and you send them to you and your child's email. This can work the same for visitation and trips. If you forget to email it take videos of times for pickups or pictures of flight information. These items can always be screenshot on a cell phone. Thus effectively and quickly ending any kind of animosity that is unwarranted or unknown by proving your actions.

This same technology can also be used when finance comes into play. Instead of giving someone cash create a bank account that has online and offline records. If you pay child support, let it come directly out of the check. That way there is no conversation or argument about what is going to where or when. The reasoning behind this to minimize all unnecessary adverse situations that take away time from enjoying parenting. Because in today's society "cash is king." Though this may be an aggravating situation, it is a necessary evil to get past. The less there is to nitpick about lessens the probability of any animosity.

Now let's use technology for more positive scenarios. When you take trips, events, parties, experiences that your child will relish for the rest of their lives, and any other great milestone. A smart phone and all of its devices is the perfect tool for all of these things. We normally see people with their phones taking pictures and video of any kind of scenario. This is part of the social media craze that we have in society. So just like anybody else who wants to get on

Facebook or Instagram and take pictures or videos you can do the same. Videotape a child's game, recital, graduation, videogame win or lose, or any other hilarious experience that life may bring to you. There are numerous times when being a proud parent can be captured right in the moment in real time. Everybody remembers the first steps or the first words maybe even the potty dance. Some of these things may seem small in the beginning but they add up to all of the great memories of being a parent and also the great situations that your child evolved from. Which is always confirmation and validation for why we love being parents.

Technology can also be a way to keep tabs on your child. When it comes to their whereabouts and their interactions in school. A phone can be a tracking device or the virtual system of how most modern schools communicate. You can directly contact or be contacted by a principal or teacher on the behalf of your child via the Internet. And this is especially important for those parents who may be considered noncustodial. Because no matter where you are the safety of your child is always paramount. Also it eases the tensions of fathers in the past and some fathers in present day who have already been given a bad name before they even show up to participate in their child's educational process. This is a way to circumvent all of the attitudes that some fathers have gotten from a lot of school staffs around the country. You can ask simple questions, get report cards, midterms, or progress reports without having to deal with rude people. It has become a real lifesaver and timesaver and also it keeps you out the past situations of fathers in the past who may have gotten the police called on them checking in on a child at school. You see, technology has evolved in such a way that we can be there physically and virtually without all of the negative human interaction that goes into play sometimes. Also, it helps you gauge where your child is at academically. That way if you have to spend some more time working on reading, arithmetic, science, writing, social studies, or any other subject that your child may be behind students in. Or they just may not be advanced and it gives you the perfect parenting opportunity and bonding time to help them to that. Ultimately what you are doing as a parent is preparing them to be the most productive, effective, and efficient human being that they can be when they become an adult.

As for keeping an eye on their whereabouts technology is fundamentally great. Your children as far as you know may or may not do social media. But for those parents who are dealing with parents who are constantly on the move i.e. serial movers. There are plenty of search engines that can be found such as Zabasearch or Intelius. These websites can pinpoint accurate addresses where your child may be living if the parent decided to move without your knowledge. Because there are scenarios where a custodial parent may move and not tell the noncustodial parent and they may notify the court before they notify the parent so you leave a parent in influx, concern, and frustration by not knowing where their child is, where they're going to school, or who's around them. This may not ease your frustration but it eases the tension of knowing where your child is. In that, find things the surrounding area may either provide or lack for children out there to prepare yourself and them for.

One of the modern-day perks about the Internet is this, the ability to enroll your child in extracurricular activities from the click of a button. You see you can enroll your child in karate that may help them with discipline issues from your cell phone at work. The same goes for any kind of sport or activity that your child may be interested. Piano lessons are just a click of a button away. Which in some eyes may make you seem a bit busy but in others you're highly organized because you've given your child a schedule and it has taken less time to make the schedule manageable. You can find daycare's, babysitters, activities, buy tickets, plan trips, do tutorials online, and get feedback from people who have previously done these things. Which gives you the opportunity to weigh your options with all the things that you want to do that are in the best interest of your child's development. As a child my grandmother used to work for AT&T before she retired. One of the lessons that she taught me that sticks with me to this day is this. She told me "I can move mountains with this telephone." And this was in the day before technology had taken over the way it has. So imagine how much you can move with your telephone.

Before we move on to the next subject understand the importance of a video camera. It can get you in or out of trouble or it can capture a great or not so great moment. Understand the importance of a voice recorder. It can be a tool to teach a lesson or a tool to use for the purpose of letting an agreement be known. Understand the importance of an email address. It can be a personal chronological filing cabinet for all the memorable experiences. Understand the importance of social media. In the sense of online parenting it can show you if your child is making the right or wrong decisions that either can be applauded or corrected. Understand the various methods of communication. Which creates no excuse for a relationship not to be built and facilitated with all these mediums of communication. And understand the power of the Internet. It knows all, sees all, saves all, and the world is your oyster if you use it properly.

The Adult Judgement

Realize that your little baby is going to grow up to be an adult and have a family of their own one day. Then they'll have a different perspective on parenting and will be able to compare it to their own childhood. The memories may or may not be seen in the same way. Your children will look at you as an adult with the ability to grasp the level of effort and sacrifice involved with the raising of them. For some it will be a make or break moment between parents and their adult children. They don't have to rely on you as adults, so at that point it's their choice to have you in or out of their life. This is when all the things that really count as far as lessons learned come to fruition.

This is why it is very important to be honest with them. You don't want to be in a situation where you're talking to an adult who is unraveling the lies that they've been told by you. Normally they will understand that a certain level of candor was needed in certain periods because of their age. A relationship built on a foundation of lies will only come back to haunt you in the end. That's because your child is really going to be an adult longer than they're going to the child. For noncustodial parents when you give them your best even in the worst circumstance they'll eventually invite you with open arms into their adult life. You will be understood and respected for all the positive work you put in. If you pour into your child to make them the best person that you can before they take over, they'll pour into your adult relationship with the same amount of love and effort. So positive or negative you will reap what you sow.

You may also become a blueprint for them as adults of what to do and what not to do. They will let you know your greatest successes and failures with them. At that point you will be graded on a curve because they'll be mature enough to understand everyone isn't perfect. But it is at that point as two adults you will be able to sit down to get an understanding and explain your similarities and differences in ideology and approach. That is usually the time when they can fully grasp your story before you became a parent. Children have a tendency to forget that their parents had a childhood that affects their adult decision-making also. This is not a reason to make an excuse but an opportunity for them to see your perspective. Some things are understandable other things may be unfathomable to them. It is just a mixed bag.

You will most definitely be judged on your impact involving their financial success or failure. This goes far beyond child support. Depending on if you were raised in the upper, middle, or lower class. They will gauge where they wound up in relation to where they started from with you. If you provided them with the tools, principles, skills, or access to the things you could provide. They will be appreciative and gracious because they are finally able to respect the sacrifice. Now if you are on the opposite end of that spectrum, you may be looked at with disappointment or disrespect. The reason being is because the actions of one generation can affect the path of the generations that come behind it. There's a sort of parental karma passed down from parent to child. So be aware that your decisions, directions, and connections may impact your child's life even if it didn't impact yours. So some people have something to build on and others have to start building on their own. This is why child support can be a problem for both custodial and noncustodial parents. Because when children become adults they begin to calculate what was spent, how it was spent, and the mentality involved with it.

Now the ultimate test of where the relationship stands is in where the grand-parenting relationship stands. You see the best indicator for future behavior is past behavior. So you will find yourself in a situation where either your child trusts you with their child or they are watching you on a type of probationary period. This is pretty much the same for the process of taking advice when raising their child. If you begin to see them do some of the positive things that you did not only will it be a compliment. It will also be a sign of validation and approval that you were doing the right thing. The same goes for the opposite scenario.

At the end of the day, as an adult they will understand that you did or didn't do the best you could with them under the circumstances that you were in. If you were the best parent that you could be and still reached for the stars. They will understand what it takes to do that and aspire to do the same. As a parent it's okay to be judged by your child. At the end of the day they are still your child. But it is very important as two adults you two understand and know how to relate to each other in the adult dynamic. If you're judged well, bravo! If you're judged not as well, there's always opportunity to create a better relationship as long as you're willing and able. Like I said earlier, whether it's positive or negative you will reap what you sow. By the way, for those parents who have selective memories. Stick with the three A's and you will be fine. Acknowledgement, apology, and atonement.

The Emotional Rollercoaster

Depending on your situation and how your situation may or may not end. It can be positively or negatively, but it may be ongoing until your kid becomes an adult. A long time ago when I was in college I learned about the five stages of grief. For anyone unaware of those five stages they are denial, anger, bargaining, depression, and acceptance. You may go through those same five stages or a variation of those stages. And these stages occur whether you have custody or you don't. Viewing some people, there is a constant back-and-forth between two parents for positioning of who's the better parent. In this tug-of-war emotions may run high or low. At some point you're going to have to be able to deal with all of the factors that may make your life better or worse. As far as the grief goes. One of its major factors is believing that there is a winner and a loser in every situation. If you can mentally change the paradigm of the situation of it being form a winner and a loser into a situation that you can channel emotion and energy into a usable lesson plan. It is at that point when you have evolved as a human being and a parent and will be able to prepare your child for life.

Denial is the first of those emotions. There comes a point in life you may have to forget your ideals because you may feel as if you don't deserve to be treated in the way that you're being treated. There are plenty of parents and fathers who gotten a raw deal when it comes to the raising of their child. And part of it now comes in when somebody doesn't necessarily know what is best for your child but makes themselves an imprint in your child's life. Yet, they will never be around to fulfill the imprint that they put in place that will govern the situation. While a parent is in essence being judged from a small window of time it is your denial that you may be or may not be a stagnant mannequin that never grows or evolves. The question isn't if you're on a pedestal or have fallen off of a pedestal? The question is how long are you willing to deny the reality of the situation and move on? You will definitely need a support system when you go into this grief. Truthfully, emotionally you go through this and may feel alone. Being that 9 out of 10 custody battles are in the mother's favor this should be something that we can quickly except. So first and foremost don't beat yourself up for what happened and don't deny your positives while you are in denial. Whether you're blindsided with divorce, knew that a separation was imminent, or unintentionally created a family. The only constant will be man, woman, and child so get used to. This may be difficult to swallow but time does heal all wounds. Just don't find yourself picking at the scab every time it's healed. None of us are exempt from life so don't begin to believe that bad things don't happen to good people. Embrace the struggle and begin to accept the moment for what it is.

Anger is the emotion that you really have to be afraid of. The thing about anger is whether it's justified or unjustified when you succumb to it there is no guarantee that the damage that has been created is reversible. You can react on anger impulse one time and then forever be lamented as The Incredible Hulk. Your anger can be used to get you to barred from seeing your child, damage relationships with family and friends, make you a nuisance to society, and the most damaging make you a nuisance to yourself. So in the advent of that you have to figure out ways to channel your emotions. If certain people anger you avoid them. Because we all know some people like to poke a stick at the bear just to aggravate it. So before your emotions get the best of you redirect your energy into things that can channel the anger out of your system such as working out, contact sports, arts, gardening, hunting, and any other thing that may calm you down and at the same time serve a purpose for your life. There is no way to take out the anger and frustration you may have on the people who anger and frustrate you in this situation. A fight or blow up will only cause years of wasted time arguing about the fight or blow up even if you were goaded into it. And when dealing with your child be on alert. The reason is, people may teach a child to lie, manipulate, omit, disrespect, and encourage dysfunctional behaviors that will probably anger you. The anger may be justified because you know these kind of habits if they persist and grow will not work well with the child becoming a enough productive adult in society. Yet you will have to exert your energy toward using logic instead of emotion in order to steer the situations back into a functional plane. As far as looking forward you have to set a better example. Due to the fact that if anger cannot be harnessed it is just an enemy. Also it would exacerbate any situation by teaching your child that throwing a tantrum actually resolves problems.

Bargaining is where it gets tricky. You see when it comes to co-parenting two people have to at some point be on the same page. You're going to have to bargain just to make sure things are in the best interest of your child. The bargaining may lead to the ups and downs of this emotional rollercoaster. Because it is within the commitments of bargaining where people sometimes do not hold up their end of the bargain. Whether that be intentionally or unintentionally. There may be a game of cat and mouse or tit-for-tat just to have some kind of gamesmanship on the other parent. So even if you attempt to come to an agreement with someone be aware that the only thing you can do is hold your end of the bargain. There may be frustration of being the bigger person, the denial of I can't believe they did this to me, the anger of the betrayal, and ultimately the creation of this emotional roller coaster cycle all over again. As the old saying goes "There's 1000 different ways to skin a cat." there are many ways to change a deal. When you look in the paper or look online there will always be a sale. Sometimes the product was marked up so the sale is just the same price it was before you saw it. Other times things are overstocked and clearance sales means things have to go at a low price. For anybody who's bought scratch and dent furniture, you can still sit on it the same as new furniture. I bring this up to say you may have to be a salesman from time to time. See everybody's not willing to have a win-lose situation so sometimes you can present a win-win situation. Where no one loses its only perception not reality. Yes, it's a bit manipulative but it is effective from time to time. Could it be a downside to this, absolutely! Because just like any deal you might have some kind of anger if you feel you've been duped. That is why earlier I stated that just holding up your end of the bargain is the easiest way it builds consistency and always puts the ball in the other parents' court.

Depression may be the state in which you feel the most alone. Because the human nature is to avoid somebody who's depressed. Thus leaving individual to wallow and replay their own sorrows over and over. This is the space where you're really going to need a support system. Especially for fathers because as a man in general society doesn't view us as having emotions. It is in this stage where you may find self-destructive activities manifest themselves. It is the depression that may lead to the alcoholism, fits of rage, self-imposed isolation, and even self-loathing. Ironically these coping mechanisms are just a silent but volatile cry for attention. There is a constant sense of loss when you can't be around your child on a regular basis. The problem is that we live in the world that doesn't care or take the time to understand that fathers have the same emotions that mothers do when faced with the separation of a child. The difficulty is dealing with it in silence. You see this in this westernized culture that as long as you pay child support that qualifies you to be a good father. Yet the guidance that is needed to produce the best adult possible is often overlooked until the child is stuck in a situation where it has to become an adult and do it fast. Which is why the sadness is ongoing, because most fathers who do their best will only be blamed for the negativity even if they were systematically shut out of the child's life.

So unlike the death of a loved one you are constantly at a funeral. And the eulogy is often in your head because of the future situations that you see ahead when they plague the life of your child and you feel helpless holding the solution. One of the easiest ways to effectively get yourself out of depression is to tap into your childlike state. There is something about using the things that used to make you happy as a kid and all the things that make you laugh as an adult. You should bombard yourselves with those things. Whether it be cartoons, music, comedies, horseplay, skateboarding, or maybe an occasional food fight. Whatever it is make sure it jumps starts the happiness and joy back into your life. Because all of these emotions have to be dealt with the same way that they deal with you, internally.

Acceptance is the greatest and most powerful of these emotions. Have you ever listened to professional athletes say they were in the zone? They often say they see the game slow down. Acceptance puts you in the zone. When you get in the space you can see everything, and can see how it affects and you can see what it did to you in the past and it is at that moment that you realize you don't have to get on the rollercoaster anymore because you've already been there. You know all of the twists and turns. When it goes up and when it goes down. It's no longer something new in a whirlwind of situations, it ages and becomes predictable. And expect that you can predict what is going to happen with high probability and certainty. The thing is you have to get to the first four stages of grief first. You began to see the reason why the game slows down is because experience is often the best teacher. So look at your situation as a learning experience that will train you to become a better parent for your child. Because at the bottom of that Pandora's box of grief is the acceptance that you may have to pass this lesson onto your child so they know what to do if it comes. It is your job to prepare them for life and they will have to deal with grief in life. You see to error is still human. But once again greatness is the ability to turn your obstacles into your accolades. So if you're going to be on the emotional rollercoaster and you're going to have to deal with the stages of grief. After all, as a parent you will either be the example of what to do or be the blueprint of what not to do. The choice will ultimately be yours.

The Legal System

Let's just get right to it. Once you involve the legal system it means things are bad. The first thing you're going have to do is get a lawyer. For those of you that can't afford a lawyer I suggest you save up and have a screening process to be comfortable with who you choose. They do have pro bono type of Family Court lawyers but if you're a guy don't expect to have access to it or to be treated nice or fairly. Some places may be understaffed and overworked so the amount of professionalism is completely on the person you are talking to when you're talking to them. So in the nicest possible way I'm trying to tell you they are probably going to be rude to you. Plus, on the safe side save yourself the aggravation of being aggravated while you're looking for someone to take your case. It's difficult to make sound decisions on a clouded mind. So when you're making your decision do background checks and get second opinions.

Yes, I have addressed that men lose 9 out of 10 Family Court custody battles. But that shouldn't deter you from trying. Because there are things that you can win besides primary custodial parent victories. Joint custody is already an option but you can also win by petitioning the court to keep your child in a certain proximity. This is for those people who want joint custody that includes the parenting time in your household. So by staying a certain distance you can always have access to your child and they have the ability to be at both homes. Something like a one week on one week off type of parenting deal. It also lowers child support payments because you are basically splitting the financial duties week to week. And one of the major reasons to ask for this type of co-parenting situation is to preemptively make sure that one party doesn't win or lose and decide to move and disrupt the relationship between parent and child.

There is another type of way to approach it. You can also have stipulations put in place that ensure that you will have to go back to court if certain standards are not consistently met. For example, most courts don't want to split up kids if they are together. But if the custodial parent separates the kids after they testified that they didn't want the children split up then that creates a whole different scenario. One in which you can go back and petition the court for custody. Now this can go for numerous types of things like support systems, familiarity of surroundings, extended family, and a host of other legitimate factors. But we all know those factors can be used in court to make a point but be something completely different in the real world. So that is why you ask for or may be granted this type of failsafe. I will say one of the major problems with this is that if a father doesn't hold up his end of a bargain it leans toward a zero tolerance policy but if a mother doesn't hold up her end of the bargain it leans toward more of a slap on the wrist.

Safety of the child is one of the major issues that can make or break a case. This is definitely something that doesn't lean in a man's favor. Because of the physical nature of masculinity, it puts you in a position where you are automatically looked at as the biggest threat to the child's safety. Which in some aspects can be seen as a logical concern but in others it can be a strategy to polarize someone as the villain. This is why most lawyers try to tell you to keep your cool. Because unfortunately you will be provoked and that is an accepted reality that there is no consequence to. So the only thing that will be punished is responses. And because of that some responses may be big some responses may be small. Sometimes it's a catch 22, if you discipline your child it can be considered abuse, and if you let it slide you are too laissez faire. The difference is your consequences won't be judged by the way which you feel is reasonable due to your response. But you have to take the good with the bad and it is what it is. The irony about safety is this, a father can be deemed as questionable and may have to work his way back into his child's life. But questionable males that mothers give unfettered access to your child are not held to the same standard. Ironically those same people may give cover to the abuser of your child and you may have to do some digging and fighting to find that out. Now if that is found to be true it also becomes valid reason for custody to be taken from one parent and given to another. This is why the cover-ups go so deep. Also this is why when children become young adults and find themselves in serious circumstances when people ask where the father is they say they don't know. Because if they do know and that father is willing, then it's time for them to try different a household. Unfortunately, honesty won't be used as the best policy in these situations.

Family Court is completely different than the court system you may envision or expect it to be. It all boils down to two parents, two lawyers, and the judge. Now you don't know anybody's biases, assumptions, belief systems, or ability to read between the lines. It is about evidence but at the same time can be completely subjective. What I mean by that is this. They have a system and criteria that is already set up that is a blueprint for the factors that go into play when they make a ruling in a custody case. You can prove that you have three fourths of those factors and still lose your case. You see beyond a shadow of a doubt does not apply nor does the 51% ideology of civil court. So you are ultimately in a completely different space. Also take into consideration that men are socially seen as the breadwinners so by default they are the first persons to financially be responsible for childhood provision. Which in a way is understandable, but also a crutch. That's why being productive can be used against you.

Financially, if you make more money expect people to petition for an increase. This doesn't matter if you get a new job, a raise, win the Lotto (hey it happens), or get married. Do not expect empathy or sympathy even if financially you're doing enough or above and beyond. On the flip side of that, if you lose what was your normal income, petition for a reduction. Because if there is no way for you to make that same amount of payments I can guarantee that you will get behind, you will be charged interest, possibly do jail time, and maybe put yourself in a position to be unable to be employed. And in this situation nobody will care about what's in the best interest of your child even if you are a good parent.

Understand the game within the game. You may find yourself in a situation where if you are in the male or female dominated department there may be some gender bias. Also people may be accustomed to addressing who is usually the plaintiffs and defendants a certain way, so they may approach you as the plaintiff or defendant without even looking at the case in front of them first. So I'm telling you that to tell you this. Sometimes it's not what you know it's who you know. There will be people who use their connections to help themselves or hurt the other party. You may not see it coming. You may get pulled over one day and be harassed and arrested for something bogus. It may be out of the blue but then you find out it has some kind of bearing in court. You've been set up. A lawyer may work a connection with someone in a different office or with the judge and the result is in the ruling of your case. You've been set up. People may provoke you to anger or instigate a fight constantly. If you lose your cool or even find yourself defending yourself, I promise you it will end up becoming evidence against you. And yes, you've been set up.

The most important lesson is this. In the legal system there will be a winner and a loser. The winner is usually the judge who got paid to be there, the lawyers who got paid to be there, the winner of the case who paid for a victory, and depending on the situation the child. The loser is usually the person who lost the case, the family of the person who lost the case, and depending on the situation the child. But in normal instances the situation is this, a court may give you guidelines to go by some of those guidelines may actually be in your child's best interest, but those guidelines will never replace the love a parent gives to their child. The Legal system is merely a temporary entity. It will only be there for your child if you call on it to be there. So ultimately you have the power of influence even under legal guidelines. With or without a ruling you are the parents. So if you are in the best interest of your child then you do what's in the best interest of your child. Because the judge won't be in the black robe. The judge will be in the mirror or in the eyes of your child as an adult.

Time Flies

Do you remember as a kid your parents telling you that time flies? They told you one day you're going to wake up and things in your childhood will seem like it was just yesterday. When you first went to high school they told you that the years go by fast. Some of us listened some of us didn't. By the time it was over and we went to college we understood the process. This same process goes for parenting. It was just yesterday you were kid, it was just yesterday you were a teenager, it was just yesterday you were young adults, and it was just yesterday when your baby was just a baby. The thing we all have to realize is we can get caught up in the back and forth, but at the end of the day it'll be over before you know it. There is a book called *Don't Sweat The Small Stuff* and I think it's apropos and absolutely right. If you want to argue and fight every day about meaningless feelings than waste your time. But I can guarantee you that you will wake up one day and realize all of the opportunities and moments you've missed sweating the small stuff.

Attack the issues. Just as you will grow older your child will grow older. It may be an emotional rollercoaster, there may be a few bumps in the road. But do your best to attack the issues that are presented and not your child who may be exhibiting dysfunctional behavior that you may or may not have caused. What is most important to you? To be right or to be the right parent for the job. If you're a child who has grown up and you have told your parent's the things that you missed or didn't get that didn't cost anything but time. The lessons that you may not have wanted to learn on your own. You see there's a big difference between a person who has been told and a person who has been shown the right way to go and chose otherwise. Then there is a person who's never been told and/or never been shown but has to figure it out on their own. Time is the one thing that we can never get back. So in order to respect the way time works we have to respect how fast it passes. So for instance, if you're in hostile situation ask yourself will this particular situation really have any kind of significant effect on my life or my child's life in the next five years? If the answer is yes, you need to devise a plan to attack the issue. If the answer is no, you don't need to waste time being hostile about frivolous things.

Manage your time in the most efficient way that yields the highest positive results of parenting. What I mean by that is this, you do not have to be a smothering individual to be the best parent you can be. Take advantage of some of the sink or swim moments that are necessary for your child to grow up. Take advantage of telling them the absolute truth and let the principles of that truth play out in life for them to see it with their own eyes. Take advantage of teaching them something and walking away to see if it interests them to the point that they are self-motivated to master it. Take advantage of showing someone how to do things the hard way because it correlates with longevity and if they choose to take shortcuts explain to them the probability of having short term results.

Have you ever caught yourself staring at your child in amazement of how fast they've grown? Every few months you need to buy new clothes and every few years you need to watch their new favorite show. Well the interesting thing about it, is that they are in amazement watching you grow also. Because your new interests and endeavors began to spark new ideas and options on which direction they would like to go in their own lives. You see sometimes we seem to forget all of the things that we liked and disliked about our own childhood. And it is in that space, where we learned from our parent's mistakes or we're dooming our children by repeating them. Due to the fact that most childhood experiences have a long-lasting if not lifetime effect on your adult personality. So if you were to be honest with yourself in addressing not the story you made your childhood to be in your mind. Rather the reality and perspectives of all of the people involved with you to get a full picture. It might not only help you to be fully self-actualized but also parent and love from a different vantage point. Because time heals all wounds but that doesn't mean the scars don't exist.

One of the biggest lessons you're going to have to face is teaching a child who has all the time in the world to respect time. We all felt invincible and immortal when we were young. The thing about that was we also saw the differences between the people who were the producers and procrastinators. The do as I say not as I do culture is one of the procrastinator. The I am going to teach you how to fish culture is one of the producers. Now the time lesson of this will simply be learned by watching and observing how you as a parent operate. Organized people are organized because it's the best way to maximize your time. Which is the reverse for disorganized people who always seem disheveled because they are always pressed for time. For example, if your kid wants to go to an event and it means the world to them at that moment. When you are organized you can get to the event on time, enjoy the ambience, and probably have a lifelong memory. But if you are disorganized you'll probably be late or you couldn't take them, and possibly turn their dream day into a nightmare. This is something I noticed over the years just dealing with people.

And since time waits for no one. You might want to look into how much time your child puts into doing something that is meaningless. Video games are fun, but you shouldn't be playing them for ridiculous amount of time. Looking good and dressing nice is important but it doesn't take forever to do. Texting and social media is also a great way to communicate but it becomes a problem when you can't talk to the person in front of you. Watching TV is perfectly fine but you may want to explain the difference between fantasy and reality. Extracurricular activities are great to do but you don't want to master one thing in a multifaceted world. I find that one of the easiest ways to get this point across is to let your child learn you. What you may do for living is not and has never been your totality as a human being. You see you're at a great advantage because you know more about your child than your child knows about you. If you look back into your own past you may find the time when you thought you were born with a certain gift, and you found out it was something that your parents were good at but you never saw them do it. It is in those moments where similarity creates an opportunity for a bond to form in a moment in time where the flying of time will stop for love and unity.

Tough Love Is Still Love

As a parent it goes with the territory to be a disciplinarian. There are going to be situations that you have to put your foot down and let your child know who is boss. Sometimes you may feel like your hands are tied because people can spin discipline into abuse. Nevertheless, you have to introduce your child to the workings of the real world. Just because you have to correct the behavior that doesn't mean it doesn't it comes from a place of love. We've seen it time and time again in our own lives where some surly individual had to teach us something the hard way so we would get it and never forget it. When it was all said and done we may not have liked it but we were grateful that it happened and we got the point and appreciated it.

The same goes for teaching the life lessons that you will have to teach your child. There is no shame in teaching anyone that all situations have positive or negative consequences. For every action there is an equal and opposite reaction. These hard lessons are meant to educate and intellectually evolve your child into an adult. Normally manners are where this tough love starts. The importance of please and thank you are the building blocks for healthy communication. So there should be no guilt when reprimanding your child for not exhibiting proper manners. After all they are an extension of you and what you taught them when they go out into the public. I would dare say the growing arrogance and entitlement that is pervasive in modern day society is partly rooted in the lack of tough love and respect when raising a child. Let us be honest with each other for one minute. Would you really go into to a restaurant and be belligerent to your server and chef and not in the back of your mind think they may do something to this food? If you're one of those people who feel as if you can talk to anybody in a disrespectful manner and there will be no repercussions, then you probably are extremely delusional. When you walk into a person's home you follow their rules. So the same has to be taught for the rules of society. So what if your child doesn't like discipline. If you don't teach them cause-and-effect than I can guarantee you law enforcement at some point will. Also look at the hypocrisy of the society that we live in. The same people who will tell you not to discipline your children or try to interject an ineffective parenting style are normally the same people complaining about young adults lacking discipline and respect.

Let's discuss the everyone is a winner mentality. Tough love is being honest enough to tell your child you don't get a trophy for showing up. In life there will be winners and losers. When we were coming up the old sports quote was "The thrill of victory and the agony of defeat." You see there was no "The pride of just showing up." In life you will win some and you will lose some. That is an inescapable inevitability. So there will be certain situations that will be fair and others that will not be fair, that is a normal part of life. Sometimes you win things fair and square and other times you may be cheated out of something. We have all had to deal with this at some point and we cannot shelter our children from the reality of the world that we and they will live in. We all partake in watching sports. In those sports we can recognize the shenanigans but except the outcome. Nobody plays for second place. Nobody wants to be mediocre. Everyone is committed to being the best even if it doesn't work out in that way. You see a true winner is able to deal with adversity and persevere through it to perform at a high level and complete the task presented. We need to expect the same things from our children. Do not get in the habit of giving easy ways out and making excuses because they will eventually make up the easy excuses to get out of finishing things.

You may have to take the same approach as the military sometimes. Life is a series of battles and within those battles you will have to make tough choices. In order to win the war, you will have to endure various will testing obstacles. So because of the severity of the circumstance your commanding officer has no time to coddle your emotions. And just like that commanding officer you will not have time to coddle your child's emotions while preparing them for the battles in life. There was a particular scene from the movie Jarhead. It was a training exercise where the soldiers had to crawl under barb wire while live ammunition was being shot over their heads. The one major rule was, do not stand up. One soldier decided to freak out and stand up as if the ammunition would stop for him. Well of course bullets don't work that way. So in the same frame of thought life doesn't work that way. You cannot throw a tantrum and expect the whole world to stop because you feel more important than everything going on around you. You as a parent will have to be the teacher of this. You see your child's interaction with the world is pretty much based on your child's interaction with you the parent. If they can get away with it with you they will assume they can get away with it with everyone else. We all know that is far from the truth. So they're going to be times that you have to teach the hard lessons in life and be unapologetic about it.

You'll see if you don't have think about these questions that some parents have to deal with. Who are they going to be calling to pick your child up from school for misbehaving? Who are they going to look at like a complete failure if your child is repeatedly disruptive? Who is the one that will be pleading with the police that the child is good after they get in trouble? Where would you be able to go without the worry that you don't know what's going to happen when you leave? How will you be able to enjoy life? When will you be able to have a good night's rest? All of these questions are the normal in the lives of people who decided to acquiesce to a child as an adult. The greatest irony of this, is that your child will only respect the parent that has boundaries, rules, and regulations. Where most parents fail and put the other parent at a disadvantage is here. You see there are plenty of kids who choose to be with one parent over the other because they love the freedom of no structure. So you have a case of heads bumping because dad may be a bad guy because dad doesn't allow dysfunction in his home. Time and time again you see the same pattern. One parent says you can't discipline my child, then they use the legal system as a guard dog to stop the other parents input, and then the child runs wild and is uncontrollable. It is at that point dads get the phone call to come get your child. Fathers know this life all too well, truthfully structure and discipline are just as important as nurturing. Because they both come from the same place of love.

Understanding Abuse and Addiction

There is something called the cycle of abuse. A lot of people find themselves in the middle of the cycle knowingly or unknowingly. Everything starts out fine and then there's growing conflict. Somewhere along the way some kind of incident will happen and after that incident people are going to try to make amends. The regular breakup to make up scenario. What's different is this, after you make up everything will be "fine" but that's just a façade. It's the calm before the storm. You don't have even to participate in it because in a worst-case scenario all you have to do is be the focus of the abuse.

The problem that most parents have in this situation is that the cycle is passed down to the child. So you might find yourself in the scenario where you constantly are starting from square one and you don't know why. Whether it's birthdays, Christmas, special occasions, and even wants along the way. You may see your child get real cozy with you and slowly but surely turn on you. At some point you will be aware enough to predict it. Getting others to acknowledge it may be a different story. Ironically if you're chess player there is great comfort and predicting the next move. The only choice is whether you're going to attack, defend, or be neutral to what's coming behind it.

Another thing to understand about abuse is that there will be a lot of secrets that would tear at the fabric of your relationship. It could be a moral issue where you don't like being lied to. It could be a parenting issue where you don't understand why there is no trust. Could be a safety issue that hinders you from protecting your child when they need you the most. These things separately or combined create a toxic atmosphere that your child will eventually consider to be normal. Unfortunately as the noncustodial parent you may often be the target of the abuse. You may be approached and even loved in a way that only a hero and villain can understand. Yet the predictability of the misplaced hatred is probably your best friend. Due to the fact that you can put a mirror up to the actions and apply them to the other people that the child would not attempt that with. This way you can handle a situation as it is and not as you assume it to be. One of the problems is people use abuse or the illusion of abuse to create an emotional response that may or may not end well. You have to think before you respond. You can call the sit down and talk with the other parent, talk privately with your child, notify the authorities, contact the school (which will probably start an investigation), or get your child out of that environment as a few options.

This is part of the reason why you need to understand addiction. Because for some children who are put on psychotropic drugs at a young age. Which by the way are usually only used in the parameters of school times settings. So if your child is only on medication during the school year be wary of the side effects. Also explain to them that sick people are not just sick when they are at school. Because this gets them accustomed to not being able to face their problems head on without some type of "medicine". As the child gets older they may trade in the medication for cigarettes. As they age a little older the level of drug may increase. This is why some have seen the child have anxiety problems that morph into addictions and become a self-sabotaging cycle. The psychological effects of coming to grips with being used by the people whom you thought loved you the most is marred with guilt and confusion. So it may be beneficial too starting from an early age to increase your child's confidence in problem solving. If they get accustomed to being able to handle problems properly they'll probably be able to navigate life better with less emotional distress. And just like the cliché of addiction the toughest part may be to get them to admit that they have a problem. You don't know when that moment is going to come but it's going to come. So stay prepared and focus on breaking the cycle when you are in the cycle. That way you build an understanding by exposing that the cycle is dysfunctional. Though it comes with a price, the beauty of exposing the dysfunction is you won't be the only person to confront it.

Unorthodox Parenting

It is perfectly fine to parent thinking outside the box. Sometimes you have to get creative to get your child's attention. In order to do that you may have to throw them a curveball from time to time. I mean what's the use of being a parent if you can't have a little fun with it. This change of pace includes bonding time as well as discipline. You will find great satisfaction in being able to have a teachable but laughable moment. So let's let the good times roll.

One of the oldest and funniest ways is to have a game night. I don't care if it's a board game or sports. Either way the competitive juices along with the opportunity to be on the winning or losing end of dinner time trash talk is fun. Some of us still have the occasional wrestling match with the baby. You two get to be your favorite character for the night and slug it out for the belt. To make it more interesting make sure you go get a championship belt. You'll be surprised at the amount of laughs you get while eating dinner with the heavyweight championship of the world on your shoulder. There's just something about the freedom of giving into childhood imagination. Because on the most basic level you as a parent just want to have fun with your child and you want them to have fun with you.

As they get older and you are not in the same household. You might want to take up the hobby of being a gamer. Get on your Xbox or your PlayStation, get online, and find your child and let the games begin. It's a fun way to keep in touch and also a way to keep the fun in the relationship. If video games aren't your thing maybe a quick video will do just fine. We've all shaken our heads at our parents trying to keep up with the times. But their effort to be open enough to try something new was always flattering. So maybe it's time to be like those old fogeys. And I bet you thought you would never be like your uncool parents. Think again.

When it pertains to discipline, the opportunity for fun is just as available. Some of us have rambunctious little children. We love them but we know that they're a handful. So, if you have one of those children who just gets in trouble all the time. Make sure they stand out. Formalwear all the time! It's quite difficult for a little boy to blend in when in a suit and tie. Plus, people are going to expect more from someone dressed like that. Of course they're going to get teased by their peers but the compliments may outweigh the teasing. Thus giving them an introduction to a different type of etiquette.

Another way would be to make a collage. Use the pictures, videos, conversations, and school work to paint them a picture of themselves. Let them see what their own behavior accumulates to when put into the form of a collage. If then they want to change the perception of themselves' it means changing the new history that they will make. Because the reality of seeing yourself in a collage is that it eliminates the façade of everything being an isolated or unrelated incident.

Because a picture is worth 1000 words. And of course a collage is only a mere glimpse of maybe even a skewed view but it is still indeed their actions.

Other things you can do is learn a new language together, take up painting, learn instruments, build something together, design clothing, a dance off, become fans of the same or rival teams, a cook off, get a pet to bond with together, and the list can go on and on. Just don't be afraid to try something outside of the box or out of your comfort zone.

Using and Becoming Wise Counsel

You are not the first person who has gone down this road and you will not be the last. So just take a look around at your family, friends, coworkers, and other people that you might come across. You will indeed find somebody who has been in your situation. Some of those people can guide you through the rough patches while others may show you examples of what not to do. Take into consideration that the times have changed and some of the dynamics of noncustodial parenting are different between generations. But by no means is that a reason to ignore the wisdom that you will receive from some of these people. Part of your ability to map out and execute the best plan for your child is to adhere to the advice given from wise counsel.

That counsel can come from parents. You should understand that people were parents before you became one. Though it is true that they may not know your child specifically, that doesn't mean that their instruction will not work. For the most part it works very effectively. If you were given advice from a grandparent, parent, or day care provider. You should open up your ears and listen. Remember there is nothing new under the sun so you don't necessarily have to be a trailblazer in regards to parenting. Sure they might tell you to do things that are out of your comfort zone. If and when what they tell you to do works it only means that you should be open to expanding your comfort zone.

When coming into contact with other noncustodial parents. You might want to pick their brain on how they were able to deal with certain problems. Due to the fact that every state doesn't have the exact same laws and it doesn't have the exact same culture. There may be something that is going on in your area in particular that may not be going on other places. This is why counsel is important. People may be able to tell you who to specifically talk to and who to specifically avoid. Furthermore, they may be able to give insight on future triumphs or obstacles that you may encounter along the way. If you're lucky someone may give you a blueprint of their old plan of action that you can revise them build on to your own.

When dealing with education find a way to get involved and listen to the professionals. A teacher can not only teach your child but they can also teach you how to teach your child. If your child is getting good grades obviously they are doing something right. So sit back and take notes so you can improve on that educational foundation by using some of those same tools to motivate and cultivate more intellectual growth. Be open to learning a different body language and different tactics to get and maintain attention. They may teach you how to navigate through the frustrations of teaching and learning the material so you will be better prepared.

When dealing with your child you will be the wise counsel. You are the one who has been where they are at and probably where they are trying to go. You're going have to be able to listen to them in order to guide them in the right direction. They're going to have to believe that the guidance that you are giving is competent and effective. This comes as no surprise that kids have a tendency to not follow instructions completely. But as the wiser of the two, you can also lay out the advantages or disadvantages of improvising the plan. It is perfectly okay for them to learn through trial and error. At the same time, it is perfectly fine to give them the blueprint and let them see how it should look in the end.

www.ingramcontent.com/pod-product-compliance
Lightning Source LLC
Chambersburg PA
CBHW081514040426
42447CB00013B/3222